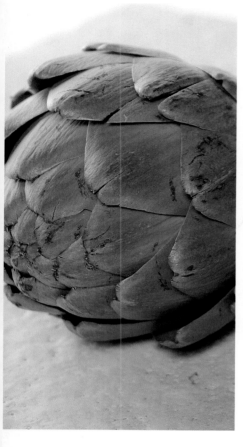

ISBN 979-8-218-05416-8

Printed in China

JUDD SERVIDIO

SALT VANILLA

A COOK'S BOOK
of edible art with stories

www.saltvanilla.com

Foreword

I crossed paths with Chef Judd Servidio more than a decade ago after he stopped by one night when we needed a guest chef. I was out of town at the time, but my wife, Eloise, called me and said, "You're not going to believe this guest chef we have here tonight; he's amazing," and I said if he's that good, invite him back when I'm home. Chef Judd came back to cook for us: I saw the care with which the meal was prepared, I saw how artfully it was placed and displayed on the plates, and most importantly, I experienced how amazing the taste was. I knew right away that this man was going nowhere except right here to our home. That was 14 years ago, and Chef Judd is still our chef today.

He has served some of the most famous people on the planet, including politicians, musicians, actors, and dignitaries – friends of ours who came to our home to eat. He has also served and exchanged meals with some of the top chefs in the world. I'll never forget the time we went to Wolfgang Puck's grand opening just outside of Beaver Creek where Wolfgang cooked for us. We had invited him to come to our house earlier in the day for appetizers. Judd got to cook for the famous Wolfgang Puck, who said to me, "He is one hell of a good chef; you've got a good one there!"

The world is now going to be exposed to the incredible culinary magic of Chef Judd Servidio with this book of his recipes. Many times we'll have a meal and I'll say, "Judd, put this one in your book. It's different from anything anyone has tasted before and it's incredible!" Chef Judd's recipes are often surprisingly inexpensive to make. They look good, taste good, and are good for you. That is an amazing thing – nearly all of his recipes are good for you! Whether you're a vegetarian, a fish eater, or a meat eater, this book has something for you.

My family and I highly recommend this book. In fact, I'm going to be buying quite a few copies to share with my business associates! All of the recipes in it are amazing, and I know you're going to have fun trying them out.

Peace, Love, & Happiness,

John Paul DeJoria

Co-Founder, Chairman of the Board, John Paul Mitchell Systems
Co-Founder, Chairman Emeritus, The Patron Spirits Company
Global Philanthropist

About this book

Like all cookbooks, this one has been a labor of love. Throughout the last decade, I have had the privilege of cooking for one of the world's most generous and loving families. This cookbook is a collection of many of the recipes I created while cooking for the DeJoria family as their personal chef.

John Paul (JP) and Eloise DeJoria live a big life. I'm continually called on to create menus for everything, ranging from family dinners to corporate lunches. I've prepared food for elegant parties, and even for entertaining royalty. It is my pleasure to share my recipes and also to offer a glimpse into my world.

We eat with our eyes first! I have enjoyed creating food that is visually pleasing and delicious! But don't let presentation scare you away from trying some of these dishes. Many of them are not as labor-intensive as they might appear.

Recipes are but a roadmap to send you down a culinary path. Feel free to stray from that path and substitute ingredients that appeal to your likes, tastes, and preferences. Most of the recipes, unless otherwise specified, are scaled for four servings.

It is my desire to help home cooks feel confident making *elevated* everyday food. That is my style of cooking. It is with absolute joy that I share this cookbook. Welcome to my table!

Table of Contents

"Stories from the kitchen" sprinkled throughout

My Approach

The world changed in 2020, and the food industry changed with it. The desire for fresh, clean food is now driving our decisions about what we put into our bodies.

When it comes to food, good health is the major consideration for my employer and me. I choose the best quality ingredients available, and organic foods comprise 99 percent of what I buy. I shop for sustainable fish and organic or grass-fed meats, and I frequent local farmers markets. It is essential to have a fully stocked pantry with nuts, legumes, dried fruits, grains, and flours. And don't forget the preserves!

I am especially fortunate to hand pick my produce from lush, organic gardens. I love planning meals around what is in season. If you have the resources for a home garden or have a CSA (community-supported agriculture) program near you, I highly recommend both. Also, planting a small herb garden would provide a wonderful resource for your cooking.

In planning what I want to cook each day, I start with a quick inventory of food on hand. That inventory guides my decisions toward the direction I end up taking. I incorporate different cooking techniques, flavors, textures, and spices to create interesting, healthy meals for the DeJorias. After all, they dine at the best restaurants around the world. That's pretty stiff competition! To compete, my meals must look and taste as good, and they must be as healthy as possible. It's not an easy task, but one that challenges me day in and day out.

I am often asked what inspires me. Like you, I find inspiration from magazines as well as the many great meals I've eaten – be it at restaurants or simply at a friend's house. But more often than not, my ideas are ingredient-driven and come from my desire to create. A lot of dishes start with what is in the fridge, the garden, and the pantry — whether fresh ingredients or leftovers. This is truly where the magic begins!

My Journey

Two meals were significant in starting me on my culinary journey. My first experience with fine dining happened when I was eight. My family had travelled to London to visit my Aunt Bea and Uncle Duke. They dined out often and had dinner at the Dorchester every Sunday night. It was there that I ordered my first smoked salmon with capers, and I absolutely loved it. I still order it every chance I get.

The second meal was also with my aunt and uncle, this time in Switzerland. We ordered raclette. I have never forgotten taking turns scraping the melting cheese and enjoying the lively conversation around the table. The impression these two meals made sparked a lasting excitement that fuels me today.

My first actual experience in the kitchen came through my home economics class in middle school. I've always had a willingness to learn and a desire to be the best I could be. It would have been nice if I had had that approach in the classroom, but by then my heart was already in the kitchen.

Upon finishing culinary school, I began my professional career with a series of entry-level jobs at various places, all involving hard work, long hours, and low pay! My first real opportunity for hands-on experience was in the kitchen at the Hilton Minneapolis. After only a few months of working the grill, I was allowed to come up with my own nightly specials. It was there that my love for cooking grew. Being given the chance to be creative transformed my love for food into a passion.

My next big opportunity came with a move to Dallas. I worked at Abacus under Chef Kent Rathbun for three years, learning new techniques and fresh ways to combine ingredients. Most important, Chef Kent taught me the business side of cooking.

After leaving Abacus I began visiting other restaurants in major U.S. cities. One of my stops was at Tru in Chicago in 2001. There I had my first experience at a chef's table in the kitchen. For hours I was dazzled by an array of amazing courses and by the dance that goes on quietly behind the scenes. This was the food I wanted to be preparing!

Seeking an even higher level of cooking brought me to Elizabeth Daniel in San Francisco. Elizabeth Daniel was an intimate restaurant with 15 tables and an open-glass French-style kitchen. The restaurant's style of cooking was completely different from anything I had experienced before. Everything was so detailed and specific. This was Michelin-style cooking. Working under Chef Daniel Patterson refined my palate and improved my skills.

After years of preparation in the culinary arts I knew I was ready to strike out on my own. I had given everything to hone my craft, but I had been on this journey alone. I could think of no better place to start a new business than Austin, Texas. That was my chance to reconnect with family, friends, and faith. It was in Austin that I started my own catering business.

My reputation as a chef began to grow and my life was coming together. I met Kelly, the amazing woman I fell in love with and married, and I was finding balance in my life. That's the moment I got the request to cook dinner one night for an unnamed client. Little did I know that this was an audition since the family was looking for a personal chef. Dinner was a success. I got a call to cook dinner again the next night. Another success. I was asked back the third day to cater a party. That's when I discovered that I was cooking for the DeJorias.

It's now been 14 years and I can say that this has been a dream job. I get to cook for amazing people on a daily basis, and I have unlimited resources at my fingertips. From a small culinary program in north Minneapolis to cooking for JP and Eloise, I have been on quite a journey!.

Tools and Techniques

One of the basic tools for a chef is the knife. First and foremost, you might want to invest in three or four really good quality knives, including: 1) a chef's knife; 2) a boning knife; 3) a paring knife; and 4) a serrated knife. I like the Japanese varieties – Mac, Shun, and Miyabi are great! German varieties are also good for a more traditional style. There are a lot to choose from, but I'm giving you just a few that I use and like.

Always keep them sharp because you actually cut yourself more with a dull knife than you do with a sharp one. When you have a dull knife, you apply more pressure to cut the ingredients instead of letting the knife do the work for you. The knife can then skip off the food and onto your hand or fingers.

Other tools you will need for some of these recipes are: 1) a peeler; 2) a micro plane; 3) a mandolin; 4) a pasta machine and attachments; 5) a ricer; 6) a cryovac or other food-saver machine; 7) a Vitamix or other quality blender; 8) an iSi Gourmet Whip; 9) a set of 12 round cookie cutters; 10) parchment paper; 11) a Big Green Egg or similar smoker / grill; 12) a vegetable juicer; 13) tart pans; 14) an ice cream maker; 15) a blow torch; and 16) SiliconeFlex molds.

Seasoning savory dishes is one of the most difficult tasks because the amount you need depends on multiple variables, including personal preference. I have provided amounts that I believe will give you the best results and the maximum flavor. Ultimately, the best advice I can give you is to keep tasting ingredients as you prepare them, and then adjust the seasoning as you go. If a dish tastes bland, then season it until it tastes good. Don't feel that you must leave the dish lacking flavor because you used the amount of seasoning called for in the recipe. Be aggressive, and don't be scared to make mistakes. And remember, practice makes perfect!

I hope you enjoy the journey!

More people today understand the importance of a good diet and the difference it can make in longevity and quality of life. Vegetables are vital to good health. This section of my cookbook is the largest because I wanted to showcase vegetables, demonstrating how you can be creative by simply drawing on their versatility. Personally, I love vegetables! I love the variety, I love the simplicity, and I love the contrasting flavors!

Vegetables have gotten a bad wrap for a long time. Why has the narrative on vegetables been skewed so wrongfully? What is it about vegetables that turns people off? Could it be the way they remember them from childhood? Maybe it was the fact that their vegetables came from cans? Maybe their vegetables were overcooked and under seasoned? Whatever the reasoning you might have for disliking vegetables, my main purpose with this section is to challenge you to change those memories of "Eat your veggies!" to admissions of "I can't stop eating veggies!"

To change the narrative, you first have to appreciate the product, and then you have to understand the characteristics of each item. Second, you must treat vegetables as you would a protein. Then a whole new world of possibilities opens up for you, the home cook!

The better the produce, the better the end product will be. I can't stress that enough! The different levels of sweetness, spiciness, firmness, size, shape, and flavor can be vast. Consider growing your own garden, seeking out local farmers markets, or finding a CSA (community supported agriculture) program that delivers local organic produce bursting with a colorful assortment of vegetables you won't find in your local supermarket.

I encourage you to try these recipes and to have fun with them! Discover new ways to prepare and serve them! It just might surprise you how quickly these recipes become family favorites!

VEGETABLES

Almond Variations
with Saffron

SERVES 4

At my employer's home we have an almond tree. I've learned that there is a short season for green almonds, or immature almonds, before they become fully mature. If you peel the outer skin of a green almond, there will be an inner white flesh that resembles that of a grape. I use green almonds when they have a crunchy texture, almost like a cucumber in flavor. The combination of spices in the saffron broth and the variations of almonds really gave life to this unique dish.

Ingredients

Saffron broth
1 cup vegetable stock (see page 318)
1/2 cup almond milk
1 teaspoon whole allspice
2 star anise
saffron
sugar
salt

2 tablespoons almond oil
4 tablespoons butter
1 cup green almonds, cleaned
(40 to 50 green almonds)
1/2 cup almonds, roasted
1/2 cup Marcona almonds

Garnish
basil leaves
chive blossoms

Instructions

For the saffron broth
In a small pot add the vegetable stock, almond milk, whole allspice, star anise, saffron, sugar, and salt. Bring to a simmer and allow to cook for 5 to 10 minutes to release the flavors. Adjust the seasoning, if need be. Set aside and keep warm.

To finish
In a sauté pan on medium heat add 1 tablespoon each of almond oil and butter. Then add the green almonds and sauté for 1 minute. Ladle 8 ounces of strained saffron broth over the almonds and bring to a simmer. Cook for 2 minutes, and then add the roasted almonds and Marcona almonds. Finish the almonds with the remaining butter. Season lightly with salt, if needed. Then spoon the almonds into four different bowls. Finish with basil leaves, chive blossoms, and a drizzle of almond oil over each bowl.

Turnips, Persimmon, Turmeric, and Anise Hyssop

SERVES 4

This recipe is perfect for winter because it is light on the stomach but heavy on flavor. It combines a few of my favorite end-of-the-year ingredients, such as persimmon, ginger, and anise hyssop. The depth of flavor comes from my two sauces. The first sauce is juiced ginger, turmeric, and orange. The other sauce is from anise hyssop. These contrasting flavors give the dish a pop that turnips need.

Ingredients

Turmeric sauce

6 ounces turmeric ginger juice
(5 large pieces of turmeric
and 1 large ginger)
10 ounces orange juice
1 tablespoon honey
1/3 cup cream
1 stick butter
salt

Anise hyssop sauce

1 1/2 cups water
1 bunch anise hyssop
1 teaspoon xanthan gum
sugar
salt

Vegetables

6 golden mini turnips
6 white mini turnips
8 tablespoons olive oil
2 persimmons
salt

Instructions

How to make the turmeric sauce

Juice the ginger and turmeric in a vegetable juicer, and then combine with the orange juice. You should have about 2 cups of juice. Take 1 1/4 cups of the juice and place it into a small pot with honey and cream. Bring to a boil, and then turn down to a simmer. Cook until you have half the amount of the liquid, and then whisk in the butter. Season with salt and keep warm.

How to prepare anise hyssop

Place water into a pot with a pinch of salt and bring to a boil. Once the water comes to a boil, place the hyssop leaves into the water, and then pour all of it into a Vitamix. Purée until smooth. While the blender is going on medium speed, add a little bit of the xantham gum until it thickens lightly. Season with salt and a sprinkle of sugar, if desired. Strain through a fine mesh sieve. Once the contents have cooled to room temperature, pour the sauce into a squirt bottle.

How to roast turnips

Place turnips on a sheet pan lined with parchment paper. Drizzle with 6 tablespoons of olive oil. Season with salt and place in a 375-degree oven for 30 minutes, or until the turnips are tender all the way through. Take out and let cool to room temperature. Slice into rounds.

continued.../

Turnips, Persimmon, Turmeric, and Anise Hyssop

To finish

Slice the persimmons into the same thickness as the turnips. Using a small round cookie cutter, cut each persimmon into rounds that are the same size as the turnips. Place a large round cookie cutter or ring mold onto a plate. Pour a ladle of turmeric sauce into the middle of the mold. Don't let the sauce touch the mold, and leave a little space for the hyssop sauce. Pour the hyssop sauce around the turmeric sauce, but still inside the ring mold. Add the turnips and persimmons around in a circular pattern. Then, as you take the ring mold away, twist it so the sauce blends in together. Drizzle the tops of the turnips and persimmons with the remaining 2 ounces of olive oil. Season with a little salt, and then garnish with hyssop flowers and cilantro.

Broccoli with Curry

SERVES 4

When I came up with this recipe, I had broccoli with long stems in the refrigerator, and I wanted to figure out something to do with them. I wanted to create a gourmet look and flavor, but one that didn't necessarily take two days to make. These three ways to prepare broccoli give a gourmet look and taste that really makes the stems the star of the dish. It looks more difficult to make than it is. This is a great starter to any meal that's vegetarian, or even vegan.

Ingredients

Curry oil
1 cup vegetable oil
1 1/2 tablespoons curry powder

Broccoli purée
1 tablespoon olive oil
1 cup broccoli heads
1 cup broccoli stems / scraps, chopped
1 teaspoon curry powder
1 teaspoon cumin powder
1 cup vegetable stock
1/3 cup cilantro leaves
salt

Curry broth
2 cups vegetable stock
1 can coconut milk
1 tablespoon curry powder
1 teaspoon garam masala
1 serrano pepper

2 cups broccoli heads
broccoli stems peeled, shaved thin, and blanched (held at room temperature)
mint leaves
chive blossoms

Instructions

For the curry oil
In a small pot add 2 tablespoons of vegetable oil and 1 1/2 tablespoons curry powder. Cook over medium heat for 30 to 45 seconds to release the flavor of the spice. Pour in the rest of the oil, slowly bringing the oil up to 165 degrees, and then turn off the heat and let the oil steep for 2 hours. Strain through a fine mesh strainer into a squirt bottle. Set aside.

How to make broccoli purée
In a small saucepot on medium heat add olive oil, broccoli heads, stems / scraps, and spices. Cook for 2 to 3 minutes, and then add the vegetable stock. Bring to a boil, cover, and turn down to a simmer, cooking for 10 minutes (until the broccoli is all very tender).

Strain off the liquid (but reserve it), place the cooked broccoli into a Vitamix with the cilantro and some of the reserved liquid. Purée until smooth. You might need to add a touch more liquid if it is too thick. Season the purée, set aside, and keep warm.

How to make curry broth
Place the vegetable stock, coconut milk, curry powder, garam masala, and serrano pepper into a pot. Bring to a boil, and then turn down to a light simmer. Cook for 8 minutes. Turn down to low heat.

continued.../

Broccoli with Curry

For the broccoli stems

Peel the tougher outer layer of the broccoli stems. Using a mandolin, carefully shave the broccoli stems into 16 thin slices. Blanch the broccoli stems for 15 seconds in a pot of salted, boiling water (1 tablespoon of salt, 4 cups of water). Strain out the stems and place them into an ice bath. Once the stems have cooled, drain off the water. Take four slices and lay them down flat onto a plate or sheet pan, overlapping them a bit. Trim up the sides of the broccoli if they aren't even in length. Repeat the process with the remaining slices so you have 4 portions. Set aside until you are ready to plate.

To finish

Place the 2 cups of broccoli heads into the warm curry broth. Season lightly with salt and cook for 3 to 5 minutes, until the broccoli is tender (you might need to do this in batches). To plate, place a few spoonfuls of broccoli purée into the bottom of the bowl.

With a spider or a perforated spoon, scoop the broccoli crowns out of the curry broth and place them on top of the broccoli purée. Place 4 slices of blanched, room-temperature broccoli stems on top. Season with salt. Ladle a little extra curry broth around the bowl. Finish with curry oil, mint leaves, and chive blossoms.

Roasted Potato with Thai Red Curry and Black Garlic

SERVES 4

This little jewel packs a lot of umami flavors into one dish. There is something so intriguing about this recipe because it is really all about the potato. You wouldn't think something so humble as the potato could turn out to be so amazing. The secret to success is buying the best potatoes. They should be freshly grown and straight from the farmer — that is the key to a potato full of flavor!

Ingredients

Red curry sauce

2 teaspoons sesame oil

1/2 onion, sliced

4 cloves of garlic

1 finger of ginger, sliced

1 lemongrass stalk, sliced

1 cinnamon stick

2 red bell peppers, chopped

1 star anise

3 Kaffir lime leaves (if you have them)

2 1/2 ounces palm sugar or granulated sugar

4 ounces red curry paste

2 cans coconut milk

1 teaspoon fish sauce (optional)

1/4 cup fresh Thai basil

1/4 cup mint

1/4 cup cilantro leaves

salt

Instructions

How to make red curry sauce

In a small saucepot on medium heat add the sesame oil, onion, garlic, ginger, lemongrass, cinnamon stick, red pepper, star anise, and Kaffir lime leaves. Cook for 10 minutes without browning. Then add the sugar and red curry paste, and cook for 1 minute or until the sugar dissolves.

Next add the coconut milk and bring to a simmer. Cook for 5 minutes and then turn off the heat. Add the fish sauce and your herbs, steeping them for 10 minutes. Strain through a fine mesh strainer. (Note: If you would like to have your sauce bright red like the picture, strain off the sauce into a Vitamix. Pick out the 2 red peppers you cooked in the sauce and add them to the blender. Purée for 30 seconds and you will have a bright red curry sauce.) You might need to adjust the seasoning with a pinch of salt. Set aside and keep warm.

Black garlic mayo

2 bulbs black garlic, peeled
1 cup mayonnaise
salt

Vegetable ash

3 carrots
1 onion, charred completely
4 large bunches of green onion or
spring onion, charred completely

Yukon potatoes

4 large organic Yukon potatoes
4 tablespoons olive oil
1 teaspoon salt

Garnish

micro cilantro
chopped chives
radish greens

How to make black garlic mayo

Add all the ingredients into a blender and purée until smooth. Adjust the seasoning with salt. Place into a squeeze bottle until ready to use.

How to make vegetable ash

Turn your grill or broiler on as high as it will go. Place all the vegetables onto the grill or into the broiler and char completely. (Note: Don't worry about burning the vegetables too much! This is foreign to our thinking, but trust me!) All the vegetables and charred bits need to be dried completely, even in the center of the vegetables. Once the charred vegetables have cooled, place them into a coffee grinder and pulse them into a powder.

How to roast potatoes

Preheat the oven to 375 degrees. Drizzle olive oil and salt over the potatoes. Put the potatoes into a roasting pan and place the pan into the oven. Roast them for about 45 minutes to 1 hour, or until the potatoes are tender. Take them out and let them rest.

To finish

Cut a small slice off one end of each potato so it can stand upright and flat on the plate. Cut a quarter off the other end of the potato. (This portion will not be used, but you should save it for another use.) Season the inside of the potato with a few grains of salt. Repeat the same process with the remaining potatoes. Spread black garlic mayo on top of each potato, and then place each potato into the bottom of a bowl. Add some hot red curry sauce around the potatoes. Add chives, cilantro, and radish greens on top. Dust the whole plate with ash.

Jerusalem Artichoke
and Black Truffle

SERVES 4

This is a fantastic recipe that will blow anyone's socks off! Truth be told, this recipe is quite easy to make. For the recipe, you simply roast the Jerusalem artichokes (also called "sunchokes") in the oven. The sauce is made with sunchokes, potato, and truffle cheese. It transforms the ingredients into a fondue without any added dairy (milk or cream), other than the cheese. You top all with fresh black truffles. It is to die for!

Ingredients

Jerusalem truffle sauce

6 sunchokes, peeled and chopped

3 baby Yukon potatoes, peeled and chopped

3 cups water

3 ounces petite truffle Gouda cheese

2 tablespoons butter

1 tablespoon (or more) black truffle oil

salt

1 pound sunchokes

3 tablespoons olive oil

1 sprig of thyme

1 large black truffle, sliced thin

salt and pepper

NOTE:

Can't find sunchokes? Substitute potatoes.

Instructions

How to make Jerusalem truffle sauce

In a small saucepot, add the sunchokes, potato, water, and a pinch of salt. Bring to a boil. Simmer for 18 minutes, or until the sunchokes and potatoes are done. Strain out the water, and place the rest of the ingredients (cheese and butter) into a blender.

Add 1 1/3 cups of the cooking water and purée for 30 seconds until the mixture is smooth and creamy. If the sauce seems too thick, add a little more water. Taste the sauce and finish with truffle oil and additional salt, if needed. Set aside and keep warm.

How to cook Jerusalem artichokes

Wash and dry the sunchokes. Place onto a sheet pan lined with parchment paper. Drizzle with olive oil and season with salt and pepper and a sprig of thyme. Preheat an oven to 350 degrees. Place the sunchokes into the oven for 30 to 35 minutes, or until they are tender all the way through. Remove from the oven and let the sunchokes cool.

You can trim off any of the "knobs" on the sunchokes if they are tough. Then slice the sunchokes into 1/8-inch to 1/4-inch thickness, placing them back onto the sheet pan. Season the slices with a little more salt and drizzle with a touch of olive oil.

To finish

Place the sunchoke slices back into the oven for 5 minutes. Remove them, placing 6 slices around the plate. Spoon the warm truffle sauce over the top of the slices. Add the fresh black truffle slices.

Cauliflower Rice, Almond, and Curry

SERVES 4

If you love cauliflower, then this recipe is for you, and if you don't like cauliflower, it might be one worth trying. At first glance this dish might look ordinary, but the secret is in the sauce. The sauce is packed with flavor and creamy in texture, but without the added fat. This union results in cauliflower that "dances" in your mouth.

Ingredients

Indian-inspired Romesco sauce
2 yellow bell peppers, roasted
1 serrano pepper
1/4 cup marcona almonds
1 clove of garlic
1 tablespoon garam masala
1/3 cup olive oil
salt

Purple cauliflower
1 head purple cauliflower
2 tablespoons olive oil
salt
1 tablespoon ras el hanout powder

Cauliflower rice
2 tablespoons olive oil
2 tablespoons butter
1 pound cauliflower, riced or diced
1/2 teaspoon salt
1 1/2 tablespoons curry powder

Garnish
1/2 cup almonds, roasted and sliced
cilantro

Instructions

How to make Romesco sauce
Place all the ingredients into a Vitamix except for the olive oil and the salt. Purée for 30 seconds, and while doing this, drizzle the olive oil into the blender in a steady stream. Season with salt and set aside.

How to roast cauliflower
Place the cauliflower into a bowl and drizzle with olive oil. Season with salt and the ras el hanout powder. Toss to incorporate everything consistently. Spread evenly on a sheet pan lined with parchment or foil. (I follow this optional step to make cleanup easier.) Place the cauliflower into the oven and roast for about 20 minutes. Meanwhile, cook the cauliflower rice.

How to cook cauliflower rice
In a small pot add the butter and oil along with the riced cauliflower and 1/2 teaspoon of salt. Cover and turn on medium heat. Cook for 4 minutes, and then add the curry powder. Cook for another 5 minutes, or until the cauliflower is tender.

To finish
Spoon some sauce onto the base of each plate. In the middle and on top of the sauce place a large cookie ring mold. Fill the ring mold with the riced cauliflower, pushing down with the back of the spoon to pack it tight. Then place the roasted cauliflower on top of the riced cauliflower. Carefully remove the cookie ring mold. Finish with toasted almonds and cilantro.

Eggplant Parmesan with
Yellow Tomato Butter Sauce

SERVES 4

This is a modern take on eggplant Parmesan. Instead of breading the eggplant in the traditional fashion, I simply grill it. When eggplant is charred, the inside becomes creamy, smoky, and wonderfully luscious in texture. After peeling the outside, I smother it with a rich tomato butter.

Ingredients

10 small eggplants, grilled (completely charred)

Yellow tomato butter

3 yellow tomatoes

1 clove of garlic

1/4 cup champagne or white wine (leftover)

1/4 cup cream

4 basil leaves

1 stick butter

salt

Garnish

1 cup bread crumbs, toasted

1 teaspoon Espelette pepper

1/4 cup Parmesan cheese, fresh-grated

1/4 cup basil leaves

3 tablespoons chive flowers

3 tablespoons basil flowers

Instructions

How to char the eggplant

Place your eggplant directly onto the hot spot of your grill, allowing all sides to blacken. (Or, if you have a gas stove, you can put the eggplant directly onto the flame of your gas burner, blackening all sides.) The eggplant should begin to release its juices. This takes approximately 3 to 4 minutes for each side. You want to char the eggplant well, but not to the point that there isn't any "meat" left inside.

Cook your eggplant for about 15 to 20 minutes, until it is charred on every side and feels fairly soft. Then place the eggplant into a bowl (while hot), covering it with plastic wrap. Allow to cool completely. Basically, you are steaming the eggplant at this point to ensure it will be thoroughly cooked. Once cooled, the eggplant should be very soft all the way through. Carefully peel the eggplant, leaving the stem on. Set it onto a sheet pan lined with parchment paper.

For the tomato butter

Chop the yellow tomatoes and garlic, placing them into a small saucepan with white wine or champagne. Season with a pinch of salt and turn on medium heat. Cook for 10 to 12 minutes, or until the wine is almost gone. Add the cream and cook for another 10 to 12 minutes. Next, place the mixture into a Vitamix with the basil. Purée until smooth, and then slowly add the butter piece by piece until a smooth consistency forms. Adjust the seasoning with salt and set it aside to keep it warm.

To finish

Add a small spoonful of sauce on top of each eggplant. Place all of them into the oven at 350 degrees for about 10 minutes, or until they are completely hot. Then take them out and place one on each plate. Ladle a generous portion of sauce on top of each eggplant. Garnish the eggplants with toasted bread crumbs, Espelette pepper, fresh Parmesan cheese, basil leaves, and chive flowers.

Onion and Artichoke
with Vegan Béarnaise

SERVES 4

When I started thinking about the traditional béarnaise, with all the egg yolks and butter, I decided to make mine vegan by using Vegenaise. The sauce is not only easier to make, but it is great when combined with onion and artichoke. Pink peppercorn finishes the dish with a little punch.

Ingredients

Béarnaise aioli
2 tablespoons fresh tarragon, chopped
1 shallot, minced
1 cup Vegenaise (or mayonaise)
1 tablespoon sherry vinegar
salt and pepper

Barigoule
6 artichokes
4 lemons
7 cups water
1 cup white wine
1 onion
6 garlic cloves
1 sprig of thyme
1 bay leaf
1 tablespoon salt

Instructions

For the béarnaise aioli
Place all the ingredients into a bowl and mix well. Season with salt, pepper, and vinegar, if need be. Mix well and set aside.

For the barigoule
Pull the tough outer leaves from the artichokes. (Wearing gloves helps you not to get pricked.) Use a knife to cut off the tops, and trim the bottoms of the green outer skin, trying to keep the stems intact.

Trim all the tough green skin from the stems as well. Immediately take half a lemon and wipe the artichoke all over to stop the oxidation process. Place the artichokes into a pot filled with water, white wine, and 1 lemon, juiced. Continue until you have all the artichokes peeled.

Then add the rest of the ingredients, including the salt, to the pot. Cut some parchment paper into a circle the size of your pot, and then cut a small circular hole into the middle of your parchment paper. This is called a cartouche. It is basically a lid for the artichokes. Place the cartouche down into the pot, keeping the artichokes submerged under the water.

Slowly bring the pot up to a simmer (just barely bubbling). Cook the artichokes until they are tender all the way through. Test the artichokes with a cake tester to see whether they're done. Take them off the heat and let them cool to room temperature.

continued.../

Onion and Artichoke with Vegan Béarnaise

Torpedo onions

8 torpedo onions or spring onions

4 tablespoons olive oil

salt and pepper

Garnish

1 cup frisee

3 tablespoons lamb's-quarters

4 tablespoons olive oil

pink peppercorn, crushed

salt

How to roast torpedo onions

On a sheet pan lined with parchment paper, add the onions. Then drizzle each onion with 1/2 a tablespoon of olive oil. Season with salt and pepper. Place into an oven preheated to 400 degrees. Roast for 15 minutes, and then flip the onions over and roast them for another 15 minutes. You want the onions to be completely tender all the way through. Once they are done, take them out and let them cool completely. Once they have cooled, peel the outer skins (if they are tough).

To finish

Slice the cooled artichoke bottoms 1/8-inch thick. Using a ring mold on each plate, place the slices of artichoke inside the molds to create an even layer of sliced artichokes. I season them with a touch of salt. Then take 1 to 2 tablespoons of the béarnaise aioli and spread it all over the sliced artichokes. Cut all the torpedo onions in half, season them with salt, and place them on top. Drizzle the remaining 3 tablespoons of olive oil over the top of the frisée and place it on top. Finish with lamb's-quarters and pink peppercorns.

A Tale of Two Sittings

When I arrived at work one morning I discovered that a luncheon and a dinner had been scheduled for that day. Even though there would be different guests at each, I needed to come up with two different menus.

What's for lunch?

I had the morning to work on the three-course lunch. We had beautiful tomatoes and cucumbers in the garden, so I put them to good use in an easy-to-prepare spicy gazpacho (see page 41). For the main course I prepared a salmon tataki (see page 153). White-fleshed salmon is rare and a nice change from pink salmon. I seared it rare and marinated it with soy and spices. My wife's love of vanilla ice cream drizzled with honey inspired the dessert course. With plenty of fresh lemons in the garden, I made a lemon ice cream topped with a honey tuile. Lemon curd and fresh berries were the colorful finishing touch.

What's for dinner?

With the remaining ivory salmon, together with melon, cucumber, and foie gras, I made a terrine. Not everyone likes foie gras, so we gave each guest a choice between the terrine and the gazpacho. To my surprise, only two individuals wanted gazpacho, one wanted both, and the others loved the terrine. The next course was a charred beet and strawberry salad with a spicy serrano sauce, and it was followed by a dish featuring cranberry beans and butter beans in a sauce of lamb merguez. I hinted at the flavors of India in the next course—seared bass with coriander seed, curry corn sauce, and a fresh cumin-fava bean purée.

Where's the beef?

Because the guests had different dietary needs, red meat was not on the menu. I served chicken roulade with Mediterranean seasoning as the main protein dish. I roasted the sous vide chicken in a Big Green Egg to give it a nice smoky flavor. Homemade gluten-free brioche rolls and pretzel bread were also served. Dessert was an angel food cake with blueberry and white peach sorbet, highlighted with lemon curd and fresh berries.

Going the extra mile

To say it was a busy day is an understatement! I was happy to accommodate all of the guests and it was a pleasure to hear the feedback on the meals.

Roasted Cabbage with Pistachio, Citrus, and Anchovy

SERVES 4

This recipe is inspired by the salad I ate at Osteria Francescana, a Michelin three-star restaurant in Modena, Italy. The chef is the world-famous Massimo Bottura. The first course was a romaine salad, something that you typically would not see in this type of restaurant. Each of the leaves was sprayed and layered with the flavors of anchovy, citrus, and pistachio. I was blown away by the simplicity of the salad and yet the complexity of the flavors. In the following recipe, I use the cabbage as the vehicle, with some added twists, to drive my take on Massimo's romaine salad.

Ingredients

Cabbage

3 small baby cabbages, blanched twice and then grilled

3 tablespoons olive oil

1/2 teaspoon salt

Fennel-tangerine purée

4 tablespoons butter

4 tablespoons olive oil

1 leek, sliced using only the white portion

1 fennel, sliced

1 tangerine, zested

1 1/2 cups tangerine juice

3 tablespoons cream

salt

Instructions

How to cook cabbage

Blanch the cabbages whole for 3 to 4 minutes. Take them out of the water and let them cool. Then cut them in half and blanch them again for 3 to 4 minutes. Take them out of the water and place them face down onto a plate. When the cabbages have completely cooled, add 3 tablespoons of olive oil and season them with 1/2 teaspoon of salt. Grill them for 2 to 3 minutes just to add a little grill-and-smoky flavor. Set aside to cool.

How to make fennel-tangerine purée

In a small saucepot on medium heat add 2 tablespoons each of butter and olive oil. Add the leek, fennel, and 2 pinches of salt to the vegetables. Cover and cook for 10 minutes, allowing the vegetables to cook but not to brown, and then add your zest and tangerine juice.

Bring to a simmer and cook for 10 minutes. Add the cream and cook for 3 minutes. Place everything into a Vitamix or other blender and purée until smooth. I add a little more butter and olive oil to smooth out the sauce and to make it a little richer.

Season with salt and set aside to cool. When the sauce reaches room temperature, pour it into a squirt bottle.

Pistachio butter

1 cup pistachios, roasted

1 cup cream

1 cup milk

1/2 cup parsley leaves

Garnishes

anchovy paste (store-bought,
or make your own)

olive oil

cabbage microgreens

chive blossoms

Espelette pepper or cayenne pepper

How to make pistachio butter

Place the pistachios, cream, and milk into a pot. Bring to a boil and turn down to a light simmer. Simmer for 30 minutes, then strain out the liquid.

Place the pistachios into a blender with the parsley leaves. Add roughly 1/2 cup of liquid back into the blender. Blend until completely smooth. (You might need to add more liquid if what you have is too thick.) Season with salt and place into a squirt bottle.

To finish

Place the cabbage into the oven at 400 degrees for 3 to 5 minutes just to warm it up. Take it out and add dots of pistachio butter, fennel-tangerine purée, and anchovy paste all over the cabbage.

Use only a small amount of the anchovy paste because of its strong flavor. Then drizzle the cabbage with olive oil. Garnish with cabbage microgreens, chive blossoms, and Espelette pepper or cayenne pepper.

Roasted Cabbage with Za'atar, Fig, and Roasted Garlic Yogurt

SERVES 8

Roasting cabbage is one of the easiest ways to add depth of flavor to an otherwise mediocre vegetable. Za'atar, a Mediterranean spice composed of thyme, sumac, and sesame seeds, really transforms the brassica. Figs, together with the yogurt sauce, are the key to making this dish shine.

Ingredients

Roasted cabbage

1 head of green cabbage, cut into eighths
10 tablespoons olive oil
2 teaspoons salt
1/4 cup za'atar spice

Roasted garlic sauce

1/4 cup garlic cloves, roasted
3/4 cup Vegenaise
3/4 cup yogurt
1 teaspoon salt

1 tablespoon butter
8 figs, cut in half
2 tablespoons white balsamic vinegar
pinch of sugar (optional)

Garnish

3 tablespoons chives, chopped

Instructions

How to roast cabbage

Cut the cabbage into 8 equal pieces (think wedges). Place the cabbage pieces onto a sheet pan lined with parchment paper. Pour 1 1/4 tablespoons of olive oil over each piece of cabbage (the front and back of each piece). Season with salt and za'atar all over. Place the pan into an oven preheated to 375 degrees and bake for 40 to 45 minutes, flipping the cabbage half way through the cooking process.

For the roasted garlic sauce

Place everything into a blender and purée until smooth. Season with salt and set aside.

To finish

In a hot sauté pan add butter, a pinch of sugar, and figs face down. Cook for 3 minutes and add the white balsamic vinegar. Cook for another 3 minutes, then turn off the heat. Place the garlic sauce onto the plate, and add the roasted cabbage on top. Finish with figs and chives.

Five Spice Butternut Squash with Pear and Chestnuts

SERVES 4

This butternut squash recipe takes advantage of the wood burning oven, which enhances all the flavors with a touch of smoke. The Big Green Egg or your own oven will also do the trick when you simply add a few wood chips and let them work their magic. The pears and chestnuts are a nice surprise in this dish.

Ingredients

Dressing
4 tablespoons olive oil

3 tablespoons white balsamic vinegar

1/2 teaspoon salt

Squash
2 pounds butternut squash (1 large)

4 large cipollini onions, cut into quarters

2 pears, peeled

1 teaspoon salt

1 teaspoon Chinese five spice

2 tablespoons olive oil

1/4 cup ginger, sliced

5 cloves of garlic

4 sprigs of thyme

Sauce
1 cup chestnuts, roasted

3 cups Ramen broth (see page 317)

2 teaspoons cornstarch

2 teaspoons water

Garnish
2 tablespoons chopped chives

1/2 cup watercress

2 tablespoons olive oil

Instructions

For the dressing

Place all three ingredients into a bowl and mix well.

For the squash

Cut the "neck" of the butternut squash into 4 1-inch thick pieces. For the cavity, cut in half and scoop out the seeds. Place the slices into the pan along with the onions and pears. Drizzle the butternut squash with the dressing and season with salt and five spice on both sides. Drizzle a little dressing over the pears and season with a pinch of salt. Add 2 tablespoons of olive oil to the onions and season with salt. Add the ginger and garlic to the pan, along with the thyme.

Place the pan into the 375-degree wood oven (if you have it). Roast for 45 minutes, or until everything is tender all the way through.

Take the pan out of the oven and allow the squash to cool slightly. Cut the pears in half and take out the cores.

To finish

In a small saucepot add the chestnuts and ramen broth. (If you want a vegetarian dish, add vegetable stock or vegetable ramen broth). Bring to a boil and turn down to a simmer. Cook for 15 minutes and then thicken slightly with cornstarch slurry. Place one slice of butternut squash onto each plate. Spoon over the chestnut ramen broth. Add the onions and pears. Top with chives and watercress.

Apple and Korean Melon
with Ginger, Peppercorn, and Basil

SERVES 4

If you ever visit Malibu on a Sunday, you must go to the farmers market. Some of the best fruit I've ever tasted comes from this market. Beautiful Korean melons from this market provide the basis for this simple, light bite. These melons are deceivingly delicious. They have a crunchiness like cucumber, and a sweetness like pear.

Ingredients

Ginger honey sauce

1 tablespoon fresh ginger, peeled

2 tablespoons honey

1/3 cup white balsamic vinegar (gourmet blends)

1/2 cup Vegenaise

1/4 cup olive oil

salt

2 apples, peeled and sliced thin

1 Korean melon, peeled and sliced thin

Garnish

1 teaspoon fleur de sel

2 tablespoons pink peppercorns, crushed

1/4 cup basil leaves and flowers

Instructions

How to make the honey ginger sauce

Place everything except the olive oil into a Vitamix. Purée for 15 seconds and then drizzle in the olive oil. Season with salt and set aside.

To finish

Peel the apples and slice them thin with a mandoline. Repeat the same process with the Korean melon. Trim the apple and melon edges so that the fruit has a rectangular shape, then place the apple and melon slices on top of each other in alternate layers. Add a few spoonfuls of the ginger honey sauce. Finish by topping the fruit layers with fleur de sel, peppercorns, and basil leaves and flowers.

Watermelon and Tomato Gazpacho

SERVES 8

What is summer without gazpacho? I went to Spain several years ago and discovered that gazpacho is everywhere. The Spaniards sell gazpacho in little to go cans like V8 juice. My take on this classic incorporates watermelon and a bit of spice. (Believe it or not, watermelon and tomatoes go together like peas and carrots.) Gazpacho is refreshing and perfect for summer!

Ingredients

Watermelon gazpacho

4 cups watermelon, chopped

2 cups heirloom tomatoes, chopped

1 cup cucumber, peeled and chopped

1 whole jalapeño pepper

3 tablespoons sherry vinegar

2 teaspoons salt (more if needed)

3 tablespoons olive oil

Garnish

1 cup heirloom yellow tomatoes, small-diced

1 cup watermelon, small-diced

1/2 jalapeño pepper, small-diced, no seeds

2 tablespoons olive oil

1 teaspoon salt

3 tablespoons olive oil (to drizzle into the bowl)

1/3 cup micro cilantro

Instructions

For the gazpacho

Add the watermelon, tomatoes, cucumbers, and jalapeño pepper to a Vitamix blender. Purée for 20 seconds, first on low and then on high. Add the vinegar and a good tablespoon of salt. Purée again for 15 seconds. Then, while the blender is on, drizzle in the olive oil. Stop to check the seasoning. Adjust the salt and / or vinegar, if need be. You shouldn't need any pepper because of the spiciness from the jalapeño and the vinegar. I like my gazpacho a little thick, but if you need to add a little water to the mixture, then do so. The soup should be smooth. Place it into the refrigerator for 1 or 2 hours. You can use the gazpacho immediately, but I think the soup is actually better the next day.

To finish

To make the tomato compote place the diced tomatoes, watermelon, and jalapeño into a bowl. (Either green onion or red onion might be a nice addition here.) Drizzle with 2 tablespoons of olive oil, and season with salt. Place a ring mold in the middle of the bowl. Place the tomato compote in the middle of the ring and push down slightly with a spoon. Then pour the gazpacho around the bowl. Remove the ring and garnish with olive oil and cilantro.

Beets, Rhubarb, Strawberries, and Basil

SERVES 4

This recipe captures the earthiness of the beet and pairs it with the tartness of rhubarb. Strawberries supply the sweetness and pistachios deliver the crunch. Small amounts of boldness from blue cheese and white balsamic topped with basil make this plate a gorgeous one!

Ingredients

Beets
2 tablespoons olive oil
4 large red beets, washed
1/2 teaspoon salt

Rhubarb
5 sticks thin rhubarb,
cut into 1-inch pieces
1 cup sautérnes
1 cup water
1 teaspoon salt
1/4 cup sugar

White balsamic vinaigrette
6 tablespoons olive oil
6 tablespoons white balsamic vinegar
1/2 teaspoon salt

1 pint small strawberries, cut in half
1/4 cup Saint Andre blue cheese
(or your favorite blue)
2 tablespoons pistachios
1/2 ounce micro basil
salt and pepper

Instructions

How to roast beets
Set your oven or grill to 400 degrees. Drizzle 2 tablespoons of olive oil over the beets. Season with salt and place them into the oven or grill. Roast them for roughly 55 to 60 minutes, or until they are tender all the way through. Use a cake tester to see whether they are done. Don't worry about the outside of the beets getting a little burnt if you are grilling them. Take the beets out of the oven or grill and allow them to cool. Once they have cooled, you can peel off some of the burnt outer skin, if desired. If not, leave it on. The roasted flavor will taste really good. Then cut the beets into eighths.

How to cook rhubarb
Place all the ingredients into a small pot with a teaspoon of salt. Bring to a simmer and cook for 5 to 7 minutes, or until the rhubarb starts to get tender. Turn off the heat and allow the rhubarb to cool in the liquid.

To finish
In a small bowl mix the oil, vinegar, and a pinch of salt. Then place the strawberries and beets into another bowl. Spoon 2 to 3 tablespoons of the vinaigrette over the strawberries and beets. Season everything with salt and pepper. Then divide the beets and strawberries up, placing them onto 4 different plates. Finish each plate with blue cheese, pistachios, rhubarb, basil, and a final drizzle of olive oil.

Asparagus Pesto "Pasta"

SERVES 4

This vegetarian dish is for anyone who loves pasta but doesn't want all the carbs. Summer cooking is all about fresh ingredients and little time spent in the kitchen. For this recipe you'll need jumbo asparagus, a great peeler, and delicious pesto. It takes only about 20 minutes start-to-finish if you already have your pesto made. If you want to see me making this dish, please go to www.saltvanilla.com and click on *Video Recipes*.

Ingredients

2 jumbo bunches of asparagus, shaved with peeler

salt

1/3 cup cream

1/4 cup pesto (see page 314)

3 tablespoons butter

pepper

Parmesan cheese, to garnish

olive oil, to garnish

Instructions

How to make asparagus "pasta"

Cut off the ends of the asparagus that are tough and woody. The jumbo ones I buy need only a little trimmed off the bottoms because the majority of the stalk is crunchy and delicious. Next, take your peeler or mandoline and shave thin strips of asparagus. When the stalks break or dwindle down to just the tips, use a knife and slice the tips to the same size as the rest of the asparagus shavings.

To finish

Place a pot of salted water (1 tablespoon of salt, 4 cups of water) onto the stove and bring it to a boil. In another large sauté pan add cream and pesto, and start to warm them up. Next, place all the shaved asparagus into the boiling water for 3 to 5 seconds, and then with a spider or other strainer, remove the asparagus and place it immediately into the cream and pesto. Add the butter and let the sauce thicken slightly so that it coats the asparagus.

Season with salt and pepper, and maybe add a little more pesto, if needed. Using a large grill fork, twirl the "pasta" asparagus around the fork and place it onto 4 different plates. Spoon the extra sauce left in the pan over the asparagus. Finish with fresh Parmesan cheese and olive oil.

Summer Salad of Beets, Nectarines, Grapes, and Fava-Miso

SERVES 4

This recipe takes a completely different direction than most dishes with nectarines and beets. It follows the Asian pursuit of balance between the sweet and spicy, between the salty and crunchy, and between the acidic and umami. There are a lot of flavors and textures that will take you by surprise! But the complexity of flavors marries well with the simplicity of appearance. If you're looking for unique, this dish would be the definition!

Ingredients

Beets
2 tablespoons olive oil
4 candy striped beets, roasted
4 golden beets, roasted
salt

Black garlic mayonnaise
3 black garlic bulbs, peeled
1 cup mayonnaise or Vegenaise
salt

Fava-miso sauce
1/3 cup fava beans,
peeled and cooked to just done
3 tablespoons koji
3 tablespoons miso
1 small jalapeño pepper
1 tablespoon rice wine vinegar
1/4 cup cilantro leaves
2 tablespoons olive oil
salt (if needed)

2 nectarines, ripe and sliced
2 radishes, sliced thin
1/4 cup marcona almonds
1/4 cup grapes, cut in half
4 tablespoons olive oil
micro cilantro

Instructions

How to roast beets
Set your oven or grill to 400 degrees. Drizzle 2 tablespoons of olive oil over the beets. Season with salt and place them into the oven or grill. Roast them for roughly 55 to 60 minutes, or until they are tender all the way through. Use a cake tester to see whether they are done. Don't worry about the outside of the beets getting a little burnt if you are grilling them. Take the beets out of the oven or grill and allow them to cool. Once they have cooled, you can peel off some of the burnt outer skin, if desired. If not, leave it on. The roasted flavor will taste really good.

For the black garlic mayonnaise
Put the garlic and the Vegenaise (or mayonnaise) into a Vitamix and purée until smooth. Salt to taste. Place into a squeeze bottle until ready to use.

How to make fava-miso sauce
Place all of the ingredients into a Vitamix except for the olive oil. Purée until smooth. Drizzle in 2 tablespoons of olive oil. Season with salt, if necessary. Set aside.

To finish
Place the fava-miso sauce down onto the plate. Then place 3 slices of beets around the sauce. Season each slice with salt. Add the nectarine slices, radish slices, almonds, and grapes. Add the black garlic mayonnaise and drizzle with olive oil. Add another pinch of salt for the radishes and nectarines. Finish with micro cilantro.

Tomatillo, Strawberry, Fig, and Avocado Salad

SERVES 4

The garden was bursting with tomatillos, and that was my inspiration for this end-of-summer salad. It takes just a few minutes to assemble and it captures sweet, sour, salty, spicy, and creamy flavors all in one. This dish is visually appealing, easy to make, and drool worthy — what else could you ask for?

Ingredients

12 tomatillos, sliced 1/8-inch thick

2 tablespoons white balsamic vinegar

1 1/2 teaspoons salt

1 large avocado, sliced and cut into discs using a small ring mold cookie cutter

10 strawberries, sliced

6 figs, sliced

1 tablespoon olive oil

1 tablespoon pink peppercorns, crushed

1 ounce micro cilantro

1 ounce micro beets

Instructions

How to prepare tomatillos

In a bowl add thin-sliced tomatillos, white balsamic vinegar, and salt. Let the mixture marinate for 10 to 15 minutes while you get everything else ready.

How to make fig and strawberry salad

Add the sliced, marinated tomatillos to the plate. Then add avocado slices and season with salt. Add the strawberries and the figs. Take some of the juice from the tomatillos and spoon it over everything. Drizzle a tablespoon of olive oil over everything. Season everything with crushed red peppercorns and another pinch of salt. Finish with micro cilantro and beets.

Celery and Onion

SERVES 6

This recipe celebrates celery and onion. I start with large red cipollini onions that become insanely sweet when roasted whole. After roasting the onions, I stuff each one with celery root purée that contrasts perfectly with the sweetness. This vegetarian recipe is finished with a celery butter sauce, and it is a recipe that even meat lovers will appreciate!

Ingredients

Celery butter
1 cup celery juice
1/4 cup cream
1 stick butter, sliced into pieces
salt

Celery root purée
2 celery roots, peeled and diced
2 teaspoons salt
5 tablespoons butter
1/4 cup cream
pepper

Onions
6 large red cipollini onions
3 tablespoons olive oil
salt and pepper

Garnish
olive oil
micro celery

Instructions

How to make celery butter sauce

Place the celery juice and cream into a small pot and bring to a boil. Turn down to a simmer and reduce by half. Then whisk in the butter until it is completely incorporated and emulsified. Season with salt and set aside, just off the direct heat to keep it warm.

How to make celery root purée

Place the celery root into a small pot. Fill it with water and add 2 teaspoons of salt. Bring to a boil, and then turn down to a simmer until the celery root is tender. Strain off the water and add the celery root back into the pot with cold butter and warm cream. Purée with a hand blender, or in a Vitamix, until smooth. Season with salt and pepper, and then set aside to cool, either in a squeeze bottle or a plastic pastry bag.

How to roast cipollini onions

On a sheet pan lined with parchment paper add the onions. Drizzle each onion with 1/2 tablespoon of olive oil. Season with salt and pepper, and place into an oven preheated to 400 degrees. Roast for 17 minutes and then flip the onions over to roast for another 15 to 17 minutes. You want the onions just becoming tender. (If you overcook the onions, they may not retain their shape.)

Once the onions are done, take them out and let them cool completely. Once they have cooled, peel the outer one or two layers of each along with the cores. Then pipe or squeeze the celery root purée into the core of an onion. Repeat with the remaining onions. Place the onions back onto the sheet pan. Drizzle all with a little olive oil and season with salt.

To finish

Place the onions back into the oven for about 10 to 12 minutes, or until they are hot all the way through. Place a ladle of celery sauce into the bottom of the bowl. Take the onions out of the oven and place one on each plate with sauce. Then drizzle each with a little more olive oil. Top with micro celery.

A Night to Remember

With dinner parties nearly every day, June 2018 was a busy and challenging time for me. It also happened to be the month of Eloise's and John Paul's 25th wedding anniversary.

Wedding article

JP shared with me a magazine article written about their wedding. Wolfgang Puck catered the affair, serving a vegetarian dinner that evening. JP asked me to select one item from Wolfgang's menu and to recreate it for their anniversary dinner. Eloise had a special request too – biscotti. She asked that the meal include biscotti because JP loves it. Wolfgang's menu listed biscotti, so I chose that item to please both of my bosses. It was a great choice because they both loved it.

A few guests were invited for the evening. JP was not eating red meat, and I had already served fish that week. I also did not want to serve chicken. Decisions, decisions. What to serve? Earlier in the week I had visited a local organic farm, where I bought an abundance of produce, more than I actually needed. Sometimes, with so much to choose from, the hardest part of preparing a meal is actually deciding what to make! Finally I realized that I didn't need to reinvent the wheel. I would make the dinner vegetarian – just as Wolfgang had done 25 years earlier.

Bringing out the flavor

I prepared a five-course vegetarian meal based on a few key vegetables: Maui onions, heirloom tomatoes, organic corn, and fresh asparagus. I stuffed the onions. The heirloom tomatoes became a tomato-water entree. I made the corn into a cream-less creamed corn (see page 54), and I paired grilled asparagus with farro for a "risotto." The dishes looked simple yet sophisticated. The guests were amazed at each course and some suggested they were "moving in." They said each dish was "better than the one before."

Chefs in some of the world's most famous restaurants are trending towards a minimalist approach to some of their dishes. Rather than adding more ingredients to a dish to get layers of flavor, they aim to start with the best fruits and vegetables, maximizing them by bringing out their unique natural flavors. For this dinner I had thought about each course and how to bring out the flavor, rather than overpowering the dishes with too many additions.

The finale

Dessert was a colorful assortment of sorbets and the requested biscotti. I served it with crème fraîche, mulberries, cherries, and blueberries. It was a special night for everyone. JP and Eloise left the next day, but sent me a text expressing their gratitude for making their anniversary a night to remember.

Moments like these motivate me to push ahead and to try my best each day. This is what continues to feed my passion and brings me joy! I had made vegetables the star of the meal, and I was honored to have stepped into Wolfgang's shoes for this one night!

Mexican Cream-less Creamed Corn

SERVES 4

This recipe is a cross between Mexican corn and creamed corn, minus the cream. The trick to this dish is juicing the corn. With a pinch of salt, the natural sugar in corn is released and thickens into a "cream." Corn on corn – there's nothing better come summertime!

Ingredients

Mexican cream-less corn

6 to 8 ears of corn in husks, roasted

Corn sauce

6 to 8 ears of corn, cut off the cob and juiced

salt

lime

Garnish

1 teaspoon chipotle powder

2 ounces semi-dried cheese (I use cotija, but Manchego would work too)

cilantro leaves

chive blossoms

Instructions

How to roast corn

Place the corn on the grill. Grill for 2 to 3 minutes on each side, and then take the corn out. Allow it to cool completely and season it with salt. Set it aside, and keep it warm.

How to make corn sauce

Place the juiced corn and a pinch of salt into a saucepot. Put the pot on medium heat, whisking the juice often to prevent scorching. The corn juice will thicken up from the natural starch and sugars, and it will become thick after about 8 minutes, depending on how high your heat is. Add salt and lime, if desired, and then set the "cream" aside. Keep it warm.

To finish

Put the corn into the oven at 400 degrees just to heat it up. Next, place each portion onto a plate. Add the sauce over the top, and sprinkle with chipotle powder, cheese, cilantro leaves, and chive blossoms.

Lentil and Bean Salad with Caramelized Onion and Castelfranco Greens

SERVES 4

An individual at a charity had bought an auction package to have lunch with JP. The lunch was originally sold for two people, but the guest had an extra person to include. Everyone was happy to oblige. The whole meal was vegetarian, and I decided to serve the salad last, on par with the French traditions. (The French actually serve salads as the last course of the meal.)

The meal was a smashing success all the way around. One of the courses I served was the Jerusalem Artichoke and Black Truffle recipe (see page 20). This was the last savory course I served. Everyone was really impressed by the simplicity of this dish. It might not sound like something that is mind-blowing, but for any vegetarian or bean-and-legumes aficionado, this really is a delicious recipe! I know lentils and beans aren't for everyone, but I would encourage you to give this recipe a chance. The secret is the onion sauce.

Ingredients

Lentils

1 cup beluga lentils
4 cups water
2 cloves of garlic
2 teaspoons salt
1 cup yellow lentils

Beans

1 cup Anasazi beans
5 cups water
1 onion, charred
1 sprig of thyme
1 bay leaf
2 cloves of garlic
2 teaspoons salt

Instructions

How to cook beluga lentils

Place all the ingredients into a pot and bring to a boil. Turn down to a simmer and cover with a lid. Cook the lentil for about 25 to 30 minutes (until they are tender all the way through, but not overcooked). Strain the lentils, reserving the liquid for another use. Pour the lentils onto a sheet pan lined with parchment to cool. Set aside. Do the same process with the yellow lentils.

How to cook Anasazi beans

Put the Anasazi beans and all the listed ingredients into a pot and place it on top of the stove on medium-high heat. Bring to a boil, and then turn down to a light simmer and cover. Cook for 40 minutes and then add the salt. Cook another 20 to 25 minutes (until the beans are tender and cooked through). Set aside to cool, still in the cooking water.

continued.../

Lentil and Bean Salad with Caramelized Onion and Castelfranco Greens

Caramelized onion sauce

2 tablespoons olive oil

2 tablespoons butter

2 onions, sliced thin

1 cup Vegenaise (or mayonnaise)

salt and pepper

5 tablespoons chimichurri
(see page 316)

1 small head of castlefranco lettuce
(2 to 3 leaves for each portion)

2 tablespoons olive oil

3 tablespoons white balsamic vinegar

1/4 teaspoon salt

How to make caramelized onions

In a large sauté pan on medium-high heat add the olive oil, butter, and sliced onions. Cook for about 25 to 30 minutes, stirring occasionally to ensure even cooking. The onions should be a golden brown color when they are done caramelizing. Once the onions are caramelized, season them with salt. Place them into a food processor, pulsing the onions to chop them, but don't purée them. Place them into a bowl with Vegenaise (or mayonnaise) and mix well. Season, and then set aside.

To finish

Place 1 1/2 cups each of the lentils and beans into a bowl. Add 5 tablespoons of chimichurri to the bean-lentil mixture. Season with salt and pepper. In a separate bowl, add castelfranco lettuce, olive oil, white balsamic vinegar, and salt. Mix well.

On a plate, using a round ring mold, place a spoonful of the caramelized onion sauce inside the ring mold and spread evenly using an offset spatula. Then add the lentil-bean mixture on top to fill the ring mold. Using the back of the spoon, press down on the mixture to make sure it is tightly bound inside the ring mold. Remove the mold and add a few leaves of castelfranco.

Olé!

Expect the unexpected! That is a saying that has taken on a new meaning for me since I became a chef.

Mexican impromptu

One Sunday, mid-morning, I learned that instead of preparing dinner for two, I would be cooking for an *A-lister* Mexican-themed party with 30 guests. I immediately set about planning the buffet table. I would need three different salsas, two styles of pico, guacamole, skirt steak, grilled chicken, corn tamales, squash blossoms, churros, and a few other items. I also wanted to pick up some serving dishes that would showcase our theme. By the time I finished my shopping, I had only 4 hours to prep, grill, and set up the bar. And just think about the labor involved in making corn tamales!

In the weeds

Most of the stress for a chef comes from having too much to do in too little time. While I was driving back from shopping, I was frantically thinking about what I would make first and stressing about how I could possibly get everything done. That feeling of being overwhelmed is known in the restaurant business as being "in the weeds." When that feeling hits me, I know that it's simply a matter of putting my head down and digging into the tasks at hand.

Time to party

With help from a friend, a local chef, I managed to have everything ready before the first guest arrived. The night was a real success. An all female, Grammy Award-winning mariachi band provided the entertainment as the guests feasted and danced the night away!

Summer Vegetable Salad

SERVES 4

This summer salad has basically everything from the market thrown into one dish. After I served this dish to one of the DeJoria's guests, she said it was the best salad she had ever had in her life. There is a lot of duck fat in this recipe, and maybe that has something to do with it! Try it, and you be the judge!

Ingredients

Artichokes

8 baby artichokes

3 lemons

5 tablespoons duck fat, warm

Carrots

12 ounces baby carrots, roasted

3 tablespoons duck fat, warm

1 tablespoon crushed coriander seed

1 teaspoon salt

1/4 teaspoon pepper

Peas

1 cup yellow snap peas, blanched

1 cup green snap peas, blanched

1 cup purple snap peas, blanched

1 cup English peas, blanched

Castelvetrano olive sauce

2 tablespoons olive oil

1/2 onion

1 clove of garlic

1 cup Castelvetrano olives

1 cup water or olive water

8 large basil leaves

2 tablespoons butter (optional)

salt

Brussels sprouts

1/4 cup duck fat

1 pound Brussels sprouts, cut in half

1 teaspoon salt

Instructions

For the artichokes

Pull the tough outer leaves off the artichokes. (Wearing gloves helps you not to get pricked.) Using a knife, cut off the tops and trim the bottoms of the green outer skin, keeping the stem intact. Trim the green tough skin from the stems as well. Cut the artichokes in half and immediately take one half of a lemon and wipe the artichoke all over to stop the oxidation process. Place it into a bowl filled with water and 1 lemon, juiced. Continue until you have all the artichokes peeled.

Place a piece of parchment paper into the bottom of a small sauté pan. Remove the artichokes from the water and pat them dry. Add the warm duck fat and the artichokes to the sauté pan on top of the parchment paper. Season with salt and place another piece of parchment paper on top. Place the pan into an oven preheated to 350 degrees and leave it for 22 to 25 minutes. Take the pan out, and then poke the artichokes with a cake tester to see whether they are tender (or cooked all the way through). If so, allow them to cool. If they need a few more minutes, just place them back into the oven.

For the carrots

Toss the carrots into a bowl with the warm duck fat, crushed coriander seed, salt, and pepper. Place all of it on a sheet pan lined with parchment paper, and put the pan into the oven to roast at 400 degrees for 35 to 40 minutes. Take it out and allow it to cool.

For the peas

To blanch (partially cook) the peas, bring a pot of salted water (1 tablespoon of salt, 4 cups of water) to a boil. Starting with the yellow peas, place them into the water for 30 to 45 seconds, depending on how big they are, and then immediately scoop them out and place them into a bowl of ice water to stop the cooking process. Repeat the same procedure with the other peas.

continued.../

Summer Vegetable Salad

Onions

8 red Cippiolini onions, roasted

3 tablespoons duck fat

salt and pepper

Garnish

radish flowers

pea flowers

For the Castelvetrano olive sauce

In a small saucepan on medium heat add the olive oil, onion, garlic, and Castelvetrano olives. Cover and cook for 5 to 7 minutes, and then take the lid off to add the water. Bring to a boil, and then turn down and simmer for 10 minutes. Pour everything into a blender and add basil leaves. Purée until smooth. Season with salt, if needed. (As an option, stir in butter.)

For the Brussels sprouts

In a small saucepot add the duck fat and bring the temperature to medium high. Place the Brussels sprouts into the pot and immediately cover the pot. (This will prevent splattering so you don't burn yourself – water and hot oil don't mix!) Keep the pot covered for about 1 minute, and then take the lid off (splattering is not likely at this point) and cook for about 4 to 5 minutes. Strain out the Brussels sprouts and season with salt. Drain onto a paper towel.

For the onions

Toss the onions into a bowl with warm duck fat, salt, and pepper. Place everything onto a sheet pan lined with parchment paper, and then roast in an oven at 400 degrees for 25 to 30 minutes. Take the pan out and allow the onions to cool. Peel the tough outer skin, and cut the onions into quarters.

To finish

Using a ring mold, place the olive sauce at the bottom of the plate. Double check to see that all the vegetables are seasoned with salt, and then arrange them on top of the sauce, starting with the Brussels sprouts, carrots, and peas. Continue with the remaining vegetables, layering them. Garnish with radish flowers and pea flowers.

Summer Beans
with Onions and Morels

SERVES 4

This dish was the second course I served during a dinner I prepared for royal guests (see page 216). I wanted to use the bounty of summer for this recipe. With the exception of chicken truffle broth, which never hurts, I kept the recipe mostly vegetarian. I love all varieties of beans – they offer not only texture, but flavor as well. Everyone loved this dish!

Ingredients

Chicken truffle broth
1 1/2 cups chicken stock, hot
1 small black truffle
3 tablespoons butter
salt

Tarragon oil
1 cup fresh tarragon leaves
1 cup oil
salt

Beans
1 cup fava beans, blanched
12 ounces yellow flat beans, blanched
12 ounces green runner beans, blanched

Onions
2 tablespoons olive oil
1 pound small spring onions or shallots, cut in half
2 tablespoons butter
12 ounces morel mushrooms, washed and dried
2 cups beef stock
2 tablespoons chimichurri sauce
salt and pepper

1 cup chicken truffle broth
3 tablespoons chives, chopped

Instructions

How to make chicken truffle broth
Place hot chicken stock into a Vitamix with the black truffle. Turn on low and work your way up to high. Purée on high for 15 seconds, and then turn down to medium low. Add the butter while the Vitamix is still running, allowing the contents to purée for another 30 seconds. Season with salt. Set aside and keep warm.

How to make tarragon oil
Place the tarragon leaves into boiling, salted water (1 tablespoon of salt, 4 cups of water) for 15 seconds, and then shock them in an ice bath. Squeeze-dry the tarragon, and then place the leaves into a Vitamix with the oil. Purée for 30 seconds, and season with salt. Strain through a chinois. (If you want no sediment in the oil at all, use a cheesecloth as well.) As you strain, let the pulp drip through rather than pushing it through, or you will end up with a lot of the pulp. Place into a squeeze bottle and set aside.

For the beans
Blanch the fava beans in salted boiling water for 3 to 4 minutes, and then strain out and place them into an ice bath to stop the cooking. Repeat the same process with the runner beans and the yellow flat beans. Once the beans have cooled completely, drain off all the water. Remove the outside peel of the fava beans and discard. Cut the runner beans and the yellow flat beans into 1/2-inch pieces.

continued.../

Summer Beans with Onions and Morels

For the onions

In a small sauté pan with 2 tablespoons of olive oil, add the spring onions face down on medium-high heat. Cook for 2 minutes, and then season with a pinch of salt. Place the onions into an oven at 375 degrees for 10 to 15 minutes, depending on how big the onions are (or until they are tender). Take them out and set them aside.

Meanwhile, in a large sauté pan add 2 tablespoons of butter, the morel mushrooms, and a pinch of salt. Cook for 7 minutes, and then add the beef stock. Cook for 7 more minutes, and then add the fava beans, runner beans, yellow flat beans, and 2 tablespoons chimichurri sauce. Cook for 3 minutes. Season with salt and pepper, and add 2 tablespoons of butter.

To finish

Place a few spoonfuls of the bean-onion-and-mushroom mixture into the bottom of the bowl with a little bit of the juices from the pan. Add a ladle of chicken truffle broth around the vegetables. Top the vegetables with the roasted onions. Garnish with tarragon oil and chives.

Radishes with Pistachio, Mint, and Deviled Egg Sauce

SERVES 4

I wanted to make radishes the star of this recipe! The dilemma was how to tame their spiciness. You can pickle them, salt them, or cook them. All of these approaches will lower their spiciness a notch and leave you with an earthier flavor. I thought about smoking them or grilling them, which would have been fine, and maybe would have added a little more to this dish (which is never a bad thing). But I wanted a cleaner look and flavor, so I simply cooked the radishes in boiling salted water until they were just done.

I had some hard-boiled eggs, and so I decided to make a sauce out of the yolks together with mustard and mayonnaise. The result is a really creamy and tangy sauce that would go well on any salad. Think deviled egg filling. I also made a mint-pistachio butter that is completely addictive. Toss everything with a light vinaigrette, and voilà!

Ingredients

Radishes
5 baby purple daikon radishes
5 baby green daikon radishes
8 baby white radishes
8 baby watermelon radishes
2 red radishes

Mint-pistachio butter
1 1/4 cups pistachios
2 1/2 cups milk
1 cup mint leaves
salt

Egg yolk-mustard sauce
4 hard-boiled egg yolks
1 tablespoon Dijon mustard
1/3 cup mayonnaise
salt and pepper

3 tablespoons white balsamic vinegar
3 tablespoons olive oil
salt
brassica flowers
mint leaves

Instructions

How to prepare radishes

Fill a pot with salted water (1 tablespoon of salt, 4 cups of water) and bring it to a boil, and then add the purple daikon radishes. Cook them about 5 minutes (depending on how big they are), or until they are tender all the way through, but not mushy at all. Take them out of the water and place them into an ice bath. Continue the same process with the green daikon, the baby white, and the baby watermelon radishes. (You might have to add a little more salt to the water after you finish with each radish.)

Once all but the red radishes are cooked, use a towel (or paper) to clean the outsides. Since they were not peeled, that outer dirty layer should come right off. Leave 1 radish of each color aside, and then slice the rest of them into 1/2-inch rounds.

How to make mint-pistachio butter

Place the pistachios and milk into a pot. After bringing the pot to a boil, turn down to a light simmer. Simmer for 20 minutes, and then place the pistachios into a blender with the mint leaves. Blend until completely smooth. You might need to add more liquid if what you have is too thick. The mint-pistachio butter should be green, creamy, and delicious. Season it with salt and place it into a squirt bottle.

continued.../

Radishes with Pistachio, Mint, and Deviled Egg Sauce

How to make hard egg yolk-mustard sauce

Place all the ingredients into a bowl (or a blender or food processor). I use a stick blender and purée everything until it is smooth and creamy. Season with salt and more mustard, if need be. Place into a squirt bottle.

How to make radish salad

In a bowl add the white balsamic vinegar, olive oil, and salt. Then place the 1/2-inch thick slices of radishes into the bowl. Season aggressively with salt and toss well. Then squirt dots of each of your two sauces all over the plate. Colorfully arrange the radishes around the plate. Slice 1 of each type of radish paper thin on a mandoline, placing these slices on top. Add some more dots on top of some of the radishes. Garnish with flowers and more mint leaves.

Parsnips, Orange, Sunflower, and Black Garlic

SERVES 4

Here is a great hors d'oeuvre that I served during a celebrity appetizer party that was mainly vegan. I had run across these adorable "baby" parsnips that I knew I wanted to use, but didn't have a clear direction when I bought them. I had leftover boiled sunflower seeds and I thought they would be a great addition to this appetizer. I had a black garlic mayo already made, along with orange gastrique. The results of this easy appetizer were absolutely fantastic!

Ingredients

Braised sunflower seeds
1/2 cup sunflower seeds

3 cups water

salt

Orange gastrique
2/3 cup orange juice

1/2 cup white balsamic vinegar

1/4 cup sugar

1 teaspoon salt

2 teaspoons water

1 teaspoon cornstarch

Fried parsnips
2 large parsnips, fried

1 cup water

2 cups vegetable oil

3 tablespoons chives, chopped

Instructions

How to braise sunflower seeds
Place the sunflower seeds into a pot with 3 cups of water and a pinch of salt. Bring to a boil, and then turn down and simmer for about 25 to 30 minutes (or until the seeds plump up and become tender all the way through). Strain off and cool completely.

How to make orange gastrique
Typically you don't use cornstarch to thicken gastrique, but at times I do to make mine just a touch thicker. Place all the ingredients, except for the water and the cornstarch, into a pot. Bring to a boil, and then turn down and simmer for 3 minutes. Then make a slurry with the water and cornstarch, stirring a few teaspoons of the slurry into the gastrique until it thickens slightly. Then simmer for another 5 minutes. Season with salt, if needed. Set aside for the gastrique to reach room temperature.

How to make fried parsnips
In a food processor, place 2 chopped parsnips and 1 cup of water. Purée the parsnips until they have become small pieces (think *brunoise*, or small dice) and are about the same size. Strain out the water from the parsnips and try to dry them as much as possible with paper towels. Then, in a small pot with vegetable oil, fry the parsnips at 325 degrees in batches until golden brown. Strain out and season with salt.

continued.../

Parsnips, Orange, Sunflower, and Black Garlic

Roasted parsnips

12 parsnips (baby or very small)

5 tablespoons olive oil

1 1/2 teaspoons salt

pepper

Garnish

1/4 cup black garlic mayo
(see page 19)

1/2 cup sunflower seeds

chives

How to roast parsnips

Preheat the oven to 350 degrees. Place the parsnips onto a sheet pan lined with parchment paper. Drizzle them with olive oil, salt, and pepper, and then place them into the oven. Cook the parsnips for about 35 to 40 minutes, or until tender. Take them out and let them cool. Once they have cooled, cut the parsnips in half, adding the orange gastrique and a touch of salt on top of each one.

To finish

Add a strip of black garlic mayo down the length of the parsnips. (If you want to serve these parsnips hot, you can place them back into the oven for 5 or 6 minutes, or until warm.) Top each one with sunflower seeds, fried parsnips, and chives.

Sunchokes with Fermented Black Bean and Citrus

SERVES 4

This sunchoke recipe with fermented black bean not only looks appealing, but tastes absolutely divine. Fermented black bean is an ingredient you can typically find in Korean or Asian markets. This appetizer or starter course is light, healthy, and most importantly — delicious! This vegetarian recipe has something for everyone!

Ingredients

Black bean sauce
5 tablespoons Korean fermented black bean paste
4 tablespoons seasame oil
2 tablespoons soy sauce
1/2 cup orange juice
1 tablespoon sriracha

Sunchokes
1 pound sunchokes
3 tablespoons olive oil
1/2 teaspoon salt

Guacamole
3 avocados
1/2 red onion, grilled and chopped fine
1 jalapeño pepper, small-diced
1 1/2 tablespoons cilantro, chopped
1 lime, juiced
salt

Garnish
2 cara cara orange supremes
1 red radish, sliced thin
1/4 cup cilantro
1 tablespoon Korean chili flakes

Instructions

For the black bean sauce
Place all the ingredients into a bowl and mix well with a whisk.

How to cook sunchokes
Wash and dry the sunchokes. Place them onto a sheet pan lined with parchment paper. Drizzle with olive oil and season with salt. Then take 1/3 of the black bean sauce and spoon it over the sunchokes. In an oven preheated to 375 degrees, cook the sunchokes for 30 minutes, periodically moving them around the pan in the sauce. Let them cool slightly. You can remove any crusty fragments that might have formed on the bottom of the sunchokes, but don't remove the crust completely.

For the guacamole
Place all the ingredients into a bowl and mix with a whisk until somewhat smooth. I like to have chunks of avocado in my guacamole rather than a smooth purée. Season with salt and set aside.

To finish
Dip each one of the sunchokes into the leftover bean sauce, and then place the sunchokes back onto the sheet pan. Place them back into the oven for about 10 minutes. Take them out and place one more tiny spoonful of sauce on each one. Then add a little bean sauce to the plate. Place a few spoonfuls of guacamole onto the plate. Add a sunchoke next to the guacamole. Add the orange supremes along with the radish slices. Finish with cilantro and Korean chili flakes.

Avocado and Egg Salad
with Spicy Serrano Sauce

SERVES 4

In my line of work sometimes I need to be able to throw together some quick and easy meals. Eggs can be one key ingredient that can help accomplish that. This recipe incorporates eggs as well as another component — a quick sauce. I have a dozen or so quick sauces, most of them stemming from mayonnaise (Vegenaise or aioli). The sauce for this recipe uses nasturtiums, which grow wild in California for a good part of the year. They have a peppery finish, and give the sauce an extra subtle kick. Substitute cilantro for nasturtiums if you don't have them available. With the addition of jicama and salsa, this recipe becomes what I call a meatless "taco salad."

Ingredients

Nasturtium-serrano sauce

2 serrano peppers

2 cups nasturtium leaves

1 cup Vegenaise (or mayonnaise)

salt

Salad

1/2 jicama, sliced thin
(or a package of jicama "tortillas")

2 avocados

4 hard-boiled eggs (see page 79)

1/4 cup salsa (see page 316)

2 radishes, sliced thin

2 tablespoons sunflower seeds

cilantro

radish flowers

4 tablespoons olive oil

cracked pepper

Instructions

For the nasturtium-serrano sauce

Place everything into a Vitamix and purée until smooth. Season with salt, and set aside.

For the salad

Place a few spoonfuls of nasturtium-serrano sauce onto the plate. Add a few slices of jicama on top of the sauce. Slice the avocados and the eggs, and then place them around the plate. Season both with salt. Add some of your favorite salsa to the plate.

Then finish with radishes, sunflower seeds, cilantro, and radish flowers. Drizzle everything with a little olive oil and cracked pepper.

Legume Salad with Green Goddess Dressing

SERVES 4

This salad was a huge crowd pleaser the first time I served it for lunch. This recipe takes common ingredients and transforms them into an exciting medley of legumes. There are a few variations that you could easily try, like adding cheese or lettuce, which I've used for another version (not seen in the photo). I remember everyone cleaning their plates and saying that this was a fantastic dish. The sauce is addictive! This recipe will leave you craving more!

Ingredients

Cured egg yolks
4 egg yolks
1 1/4 cups sugar
1 1/4 cups salt

Legume salad – beluga lentils
1 onion charred
1 sprig of rosemary
2 cloves of garlic
1 teaspoon salt
1 cup beluga lentils

Legume salad – rice beans
1 onion charred
1 sprig of rosemary
2 cloves of garlic
1 teaspoon salt
1 cup rice beans

Legume salad – heirloom (black) beans
1 onion charred
1 sprig of rosemary
2 cloves of garlic
1 teaspoon salt
1 cup heirloom (black) beans

Instructions

How to cure egg yolks

In a bowl mix together the salt and sugar. In a shallow dish, add enough of the salt and sugar mix to coat the bottom. Then make 4 indents, carefully placing the yolks into each indentation. Cover the yolks with the remaining cure mix, and then place them into the refrigerator for 4 days.

Take the egg yolks out, carefully removing all of the salt and sugar from them. Set the oven or dehydrator to 150 degrees. Spray the wire rack with nonstick spray, and then place the yolks on it. Leave them in the oven or dehydrator for 2 hours (until the yolk has firmed up). Let them cool, and then keep them in an airtight container in the refrigerator until needed.

How to cook lentils, beans, and peas

Fill 3 separate pots with water, charred onion, rosemary, garlic, and salt. Place the beluga lentils into one pot and cook them for approximately 30 minutes. Place the rice beans into the second pot and the heirloom beans into the third, cooking each of them approximately 1 hour. When done, set all three pots aside, allowing the lentils and beans to cool in their cooking water.

Blanch the snap peas and then shock them in an ice bath. Repeat this process for the lima beans. Cut them into desired shapes and set aside. Keep 4 snap peas whole and take off one side of each for the garnish.

continued.../

Legume Salad with Green Goddess Dressing

**Legume salad –
other peas and beans**

1 cup snap peas, blanched,
chopped, and hulled

1 cup lima beans, blanched and peeled

Green goddess dressing

3 anchovies

1/4 cup roasted garlic, with oil

1 small jalapeño pepper

1/4 cup white balsamic vinegar
(good quality)

1 bunch parsley

1 bunch basil

1 cup Vegenaise (or mayonnaise)

salt and pepper

4 tablespoons olive oil

1/2 cup roasted peanuts, salted

2 ounces manouri cheese
(optional – not shown in picture)

1 ounce pea sprouts

How to make green goddess dressing

Place the anchovies, roasted garlic, white balsamic vinegar, and herbs into a Vitamix. Purée until smooth, and then fold the purée into Vegenaise or mayonnaise. Season with salt and pepper, and set aside.

To finish

Strain out the beans, but keep the water for another purpose. Place 1 cup each of the rice beans, heirloom beans, lentils, lima beans, and snap peas into a mixing bowl. Add the olive oil and season with salt and pepper. Place a generous spoonful of green goddess dressing onto each plate. Add all the legumes, and then the peanuts, to each plate. Grate the cured egg yolk on top. (If desired, add manouri cheese — not shown.) Add pea sprouts and 1 whole snap pea for each plate.

Sweet Potato
and Sunchokes a la Huancaína

SERVES 6

This sweet potato dish, with Peruvian flare, is one that caught my attention when I visited the country while courting my wife. The sauce (*a la huancaína*) is made from *aji amarillo* peppers, cheese and *huacatay*. The *huancaína* sauce is typically served over boiled potatoes and hard-boiled eggs. This recipe is my twist on the classic Peruvian dish.

Ingredients

Sunchokes

1 pound sunchokes

3 tablespoons olive oil

salt and pepper

Sweet potato

3 large sweet potatoes

3 tablespoons olive oil

1/4 teaspoon salt

pepper

Huancaína sauce

2 tablespoons huacatay leaves or cilantro

4 aji amarillo (yellow chili) peppers, roasted and peeled (or 1/2 cup of purée)

1 cup evaporated milk

5 crisp sourdough crackers

1/3 cup cotija cheese, fine-ground (or Parmesan)

1/2 teaspoon salt (or to taste)

Hard-boiled eggs

6 whole eggs

Instructions

How to prepare sunchokes

Preheat a wood oven to 400 degrees. In a bowl, toss the sunchokes with the olive oil, salt, and pepper. Place the sunchokes onto a sheet pan, and then roast them in the wood oven for 30 minutes. Remove the pan from the oven and set it aside.

For the sweet potato

In a bowl, toss the sweet potatoes with the olive oil, salt, and pepper. Place the sweet potatoes onto a sheet pan, and then roast them in wood oven or regular oven at 400 degrees for about 45 minutes. Take the pan out of the oven and set it aside.

How to prepare *huancaína* sauce

Place the *huacatay* leaves, roasted chilis, and evaporated milk into a Vitamix. Purée until smooth, and then add the crackers and cheese. Season with salt. Purée until smooth and a little thick. Adjust the seasoning, if necessary, and then set the sauce aside.

For the hard-boiled eggs

Place the eggs into a small pot and fill it with cold water, covering the eggs completely. Bring to a boil, and then boil for 5 minutes. Drain the water off and fill the pot with cool water (on top of the eggs). I allow mine to sit in the pot for another 5 to 10 minutes. When they are cool enough to touch, peel the eggs and quarter them.

continued.../

Sweet Potato and Sunchokes a la Huancaína

Chili oil

4 whole red jalapeño peppers
1 1/4 cups vegetable oil
1/2 teaspoon salt

Garnish

2 tablespoons cilantro leaves
1/4 cup fava chips

For the chili oil

Place the jalapeño peppers and vegetable oil into a Vitamix and purée for 30 to 45 seconds. Season with salt and set aside for later. (Store in a refrigerator.)

To finish

Cut the sweet potato into 1/2-inch thick pieces. Place two slices onto each plate. Season with a pinch of salt on top of each sweet potato. Add a few pieces of sunchokes next to the potatoes. Add the *huancaína* sauce all over the vegetables. Finish with the hard-boiled eggs, cilantro, chili oil, and fava chips.

Ratatouille with Panelle

SERVES 8

Your summer garden may provide all the necessary ingredients for ratatouille. If you have never heard of the dish but have seen the movie Ratatouille, then you're already one step closer to the recipe. Ratatouille is a stew typically using eggplant, tomatoes, peppers, and squash varieties. I put my twist on the recipe by adding the Sicilian garbanzo panelle cake.

Ingredients

Ratatouille

5 tablespoons olive oil

1 cup onion (1/2 onion), small-diced

1 1/2 cups eggplant (1 large or 2 small), medium-diced

3 cloves of garlic, minced

6 small tomatoes (3/4 cup diced; the rest puréed)

1 green bell pepper, medium-diced

1 yellow bell pepper, medium-diced

1 yellow zucchini (large), small-diced

1 tablespoon fresh basil, chopped

chili flakes

salt and pepper

Panelle (garbanzo polenta)

3 cups water (or stock, if you have it)

1 1/2 cups garbanzo flour

1/2 cup Parmesan cheese, finely grated

3 tablespoons olive oil

salt

Instructions

For the ratatouille

In a medium-large saucepan, add the olive oil, onions, and eggplant. Season with a pinch of salt, and then cook for 3 to 4 minutes. Next add the garlic and the chili flakes, and then cook for another 2 minutes. Purée a little more than half of your tomatoes. Pour the purée into the pot with the vegetables.

Add another pinch of salt. Cook for 2 minutes, and then add the peppers and zucchini along with another healthy pinch of salt. Cover the pot and cook for 12 minutes.

Add the diced tomatoes and cook for another 15 minutes, stirring occasionally. Add the chopped basil and season everything with salt and pepper.

All the vegetables should be tender at this point. If not, you can cook for another few minutes. Turn to low or keep warm while you make the panelle.

How to make panelle

In a medium pot add water and a teaspoon of salt. Bring to a boil. While stirring vigorously, add the garbanzo flour and continue stirring until all is incorporated and smooth. Cook for 20 minutes, or until the flour has been completely cooked. (If you still have lumps, then use a hand stick blender to purée the polenta. This will get rid of any lumps). Add the Parmesan cheese and stir until well combined. Adjust the seasoning, if need be.

continued.../

Ratatouille with Panelle

Pour the hot panelle into a square or round baking dish, or onto a sheet pan. Then with a spatula, distribute the panelle evenly and smoothly. One trick is to place a piece of plastic wrap over the top, using your hands to help distribute the panelle evenly.

Place the panelle into the refrigerator for at least 1 hour. This step will "set" the panelle. Then, using a round cookie cutter, cut out rounds of the panelle. In a medium-hot pan, add 3 tablespoons of olive oil and 4 pieces of panelle. Fry for 2 to 3 minutes on each side until each piece is lightly browned and has a bit of a crust.

To finish

Spoon the ratatouille into a large ring mold and pack it down gently with the back of a spoon. Then put the panelle on top. Remove the ring mold. Finish by grating a little fresh Parmesan cheese over the panelle, together with a drizzle of olive oil. Top it off with basil leaves.

a: wood-roasted duck
(recipe on pages 241-242)

b: Osteria Francescana (the 3-star Michelin restaurant
that inspired the cabbage dish on pages 32-33)

c: plums and nectarines picked fresh
(great for the recipes on pages 298 and 301)

d: picking heirloom tomatoes in the garden

e: black bass (recipe on pages 195-196)

f: berries and cream with honey cake (recipe on pages 271-272)

g: tortellini prior to cooking (recipe on pages 115-116)

e

f

g

Being an Italian American may have something to do with my love for pasta. Back in my early restaurant days, as a sous chef I looked forward to making fresh pasta and creating the daily specials. Since then, I have traveled to Italy on many occasions, and those trips have only deepened my love affair with pasta.

Depending where you are in Italy, the types of pasta dough vary. The south tends to lean towards a semolina-and-water-based pasta; the north tends to lean towards an egg-and-flour-based pasta. You can play around with all types of flour, giving you different textures and levels of chew (al dente). On several occasions in this section this idea comes to life when my recipe calls for adding semolina to my egg-based pasta, which gives it a little more bite.

In this section I offer lots of variations of pasta recipes by changing the sauces, fillings, flour, or shapes. Create irresistible flavors and colors by adding herbs and purées to the dough and fillings. The possibilities with pasta are endless!

Not all pasta dishes need to be heavy. In Italy I learned the importance of serving just the right amount of sauce. Whether you are making your own sauce or using store-bought sauce, strive to coat each strand of the pasta without drowning it.

The pasta recipes included here give a broad range of options and combinations. I hope you enjoy them as much as I do!

Buon appetito!

PASTA

Manti Pasta with Cauliflower, Leek, and Truffle

SERVES 6–8

As a chef, I always find it a challenge to create a new dish from leftovers. Many traditional stuffed pasta recipes use potato in the filling. When I first made this dish, I had cauliflower mashed potato already made from the night before. I thought it would be perfect for this manti-shaped pasta. Leeks and truffle rounded out the dish, and before I knew it, I had a whole new recipe!

Ingredients

Cauliflower purée

1/2 head cauliflower, with most of the stem intact
1 large Idaho potato, peeled and chopped
5 tablespoons butter
splash of milk (if needed)
salt and pepper

Leek sauce

1 pound leek tops
1/3 cup cream
4 tablespoons butter
salt

Basic egg pasta

3 cups flour
3 eggs
3 egg yolks
2 tablespoons warm water
1 teaspoon salt

Instructions

For the cauliflower purée

Place the cauliflower and potato into a small pot and fill it with water. Add salt and bring to a boil. Turn down and simmer for 20 minutes, or until the potato pieces are tender. Strain out the water well. Using a hand blender, purée the mixture, adding butter and milk if needed. Season with salt and pepper. You can use this purée hot for another recipe, but for this one, cool it completely. (Overnight is best.)

For the leek sauce

Place leek tops into boiling salted water (1 tablespoon of salt, 4 cups of water) and cook until they are tender, but still a vibrant green (approximately 3 to 5 minutes). Meanwhile, heat up the cream in a small pot. Strain the leek tops and place them into the Vitamix with the hot cream. Purée until smooth. While the Vitamix is still running, add the butter. If the sauce is a touch thick, you can thin it out with a little of the blanching water. Season with salt and keep warm.

For the pasta

Place 3 cups of flour into a bowl. Make a well in the center of the flour. Add the eggs, yolks, water, and salt. With a fork, stir the egg mixture until it starts to form a ball of dough. Then use your hands to form the dough. Add more flour if the dough is wet.

continued.../

Manti Pasta with Cauliflower, Leek, and Truffle

4 tablespoons butter

2 tablespoons olive oil

2 leek bottoms, sliced 1/4-inch thick and blanched

8 ounces nameko mushrooms

1 black Australian truffle, roughly chopped

1 tablespoon basil flowers

salt and pepper

Knead the pasta for 5 minutes, and then cover and let it rest for at least 30 minutes. Cut your pasta in half. Leave half covered while you work with the other half. Use a rolling pin to roll half of the pasta until the dough is thin enough to fit inside the thickest setting on your pasta machine. Run the pasta all the way down to the lowest setting twice, dusting the dough with flour if it is too wet.

On the third time, run the pasta down to the second-lowest or third-lowest setting, depending on the strength of the dough. Again, use a little flour for dusting. If you feel that the dough is very strong, and that it has a good density, you might be fine with the second-lowest setting. If you feel that the dough is loose and doesn't have the right structure to it, then you might want to go a little thicker with the third-lowest setting.

Once you have the flat pasta all laid out, you can take an adjustable pasta cutter and cut 1-inch-by-1-inch squares. Place your cauliflower purée into a plastic piping bag. Cut the tip off and place a small dollop of purée onto each square. Using a water spray bottle or a pastry brush, spray or brush the pasta ends lightly.

Taking one side of the square in each hand, pinch the two ends together (one in the left hand and the other in the right hand). Then bring both hands to the center and pinch all 4 ends together, forming a pyramid or a manti. Continue the process until you have all the pasta shapes made. It should look something like the ones in the photo on page 89.

To finish

In a large sauté pan add 1 tablespoon of butter as well as 2 tablespoons of olive oil, the leek bottoms, and the nameko mushrooms. Cook for 3 minutes. Meanwhile, place your pasta into boiling salted water (2 tablespoons of salt, 12 cups of water) and cook for 2 to 3 minutes, or until it floats to the top. Strain off the water and place the pasta into the sauté pan. Add a little of the cooking water to the pan, along with the rest of the butter, to make a pan sauce. Season the whole pan with salt and pepper. Then add some of the sauce to the bottom of the bowl in which you'll serve the pasta. Add the leeks and mushrooms around the sauce, and then add the pasta on top of the sauce. Finish with chopped truffle pieces, flowers, and a drizzle of olive oil.

Fava Bean Gnudi with Lemon and Mushrooms

SERVES 6–8

Gnudi is a ricotta dumpling that is treated like pasta. When I first made this dish, fava beans were in season. I wanted to build the dish around these two ingredients. I used both dried and fresh fava beans, along with their edible leaves, to mix up the flavor and to add texture. I added a little lemon to the pan butter sauce, brightening the dish. To see a video tutorial, go to www.saltandvanilla.com and click on *Video Recipes*.

Ingredients

Gnudi

2 pounds baby fava leaves
(or substitute spinach if you need to)
1 pound ricotta cheese, fresh-drained
1 1/4 cups breadcrumbs
1/3 cup to 1/2 cup flour
(to form the balls)
4 to 5 ounces
Pecorino Romano cheese
1 egg
1/4 teaspoon chili flakes
1/2 teaspoon nutmeg
1/2 cup flour (to coat the balls)
salt and pepper

Cooked yellow fava beans

1 cup dried yellow fava beans
1 shallot
2 cloves of garlic
4 cups water
1 sprig of thyme
salt

Instructions

How to make gnudi

You can either prepare the gnudi in a food processor or in a bowl. I choose to use a food processor. First, blanch the fava leaves for 1 minute in boiling salted water (2 tablespoons of salt, 12 cups of water), and then shock them in an ice bath. Allow the fava leaves to cool completely, and then strain off the water. At this point you need to squeeze all the water out of the fava leaves as much as possible.

Place the leaves into a food processor, pulse a few times, and then add the ricotta cheese, bread crumbs, flour (1/3 cup to 1/2 cup), Pecorino Romano cheese, egg, chili flakes, nutmeg, salt, and pepper. Purée until you have a consistent texture. The mixture should hold together and it should be moist but not overly wet. You don't want it too dry because that would make the dumplings denser.

Using a small ice cream scoop, form little balls, and then roll them in a small bowl with the remaining 1/2 cup of flour to coat them. Place them onto a sheet pan lined with parchment paper. This recipe should give you about 65 balls.

You can prepare the gnudi ahead of time, and then keep them in the refrigerator wrapped up until you are ready to cook and serve the dumplings.

continued.../

Fava Bean Gnudi with Lemon and Mushrooms

Fresh fava beans

2 tablespoons olive oil

5 tablespoons butter

1/2 pound Trumpet Royale™ mushrooms (scored, if desired)

1 cup fresh fava beans, blanched and peeled

1 cup fava bean water

1 lemon, juiced

salt and pepper

Garnish

green garlic oil (see page 316)

petite fennel

How to cook fava beans

In a small saucepot, add the dried yellow fava beans, shallot, garlic cloves, water, thyme, and a teaspoon of salt. Bring to a boil, cover, and turn down to a simmer. Cook for 20 minutes, or until the beans are tender. Turn off the heat, allowing the beans to cool to room temperature (still in the cooking liquid). Reserve the bean water for the gnudi.

Bring a pot of salted water (1 tablespoon of salt, 4 cups of water) to a boil. Place the shucked fresh fava beans into the boiling water for 3 minutes, and then strain out and place them into an ice bath. Peel the outer skins of the fava beans. Discard the skins and place the beans into a bowl.

How to cook gnudi

Place a pot of salted water (2 tablespoons of salt, 12 cups of water) on the stove and bring it to a boil. Meanwhile, in a large sauté pan, add 2 tablespoons of olive oil, 1 tablespoon of butter, and the Trumpet Royale™ mushrooms. Cook for 5 minutes, and then add both the cooked dried fava beans and the blanched fresh fava beans. Cook for 1 more minute, and then add the bean water you had set aside.

To finish

Place about half of the gnudi into the boiling water at one time, allowing them to float to the top. This should take about 4 minutes. (Note that if you taste one and it is a bit "gummy," then cook the gnudi 1 to 2 more minutes. This should completely cook all the flour out of the gnudi so that they are light and melt in your mouth.) Scoop the gnudi out of the water and directly into the sauté pan. Add the remaining 4 tablespoons of butter and twirl the pan so that the butter emulsifies, coating everything well.

Add a little lemon juice, salt, and pepper. Place three dumplings onto each plate with some of the fava beans. Place the mushrooms on top. Drizzle with green garlic oil and top with petite fennel.

Doppio Ravioli with Fava Bean and Cheese Filling

SERVES 6–8

My love for pasta took over as I explored the countless ways of preparing this ultimate comfort food. So what is doppio ravioli? Doppio (or double) ravioli is the result of taking two different fillings and putting them side-by-side in one ravioli. Double the flavor, double the fun!

Ingredients

Cheese filling

2 ounces Parmesan cheese
2 ounces Asiago (or Trugole) cheese
1 pound ricotta cheese
salt and pepper

Fava bean filling

1 cup mint leaves
1 ounce Parmesan cheese
1 1/2 cups cooked fava beans
1 small potato, peeled and cooked

Double ravioli pasta

2 3/4 cups flour
3 eggs
3 egg yolks
splash of water
1 teaspoon salt

Ravioli

6 ounces maitake mushrooms
4 tablespoons butter
2 tablespoons olive oil
1/4 teaspoon chili flakes
1/4 cup cooked fava beans
1 cup vegetable broth
(or stock; see page 318)
chives
chive flowers
Parmesan cheese
salt and pepper

Instructions

How to make cheese filling

In a food processor place the Parmesan cheese and the Asiago cheese. Purée until the cheeses are finely broken down, then add the fresh ricotta cheese. Purée until smooth. Season with salt and pepper, and then place the cheese filling into a plastic disposable pastry bag. Set aside in the refrigerator until the pasta is ready, but don't let it get too cold or it will be hard to pipe.

How to make fava bean filling

Place all the ingredients into a food processor and purée until smooth. The filling should have a nice green color to it and it should have a good mix of flavor from the mint, Parmesan cheese, and fava beans. Place the filling into a plastic disposable pastry bag. Set it aside in the refrigerator until the pasta is ready, but don't let it get too cold or it will be hard to pipe.

How to make double ravioli pasta

Place the flour into a bowl and make a well or hole in the center of the flour. Put the eggs, yolks, warm water, and salt into the well. Using a fork, beat the eggs until smooth. With the fork, gradually stir in the flour little by little until the egg isn't so sticky. (Take the flour from the outside and work into the middle of the egg mixture.)

Using your hands instead of the fork, begin forming the dough by folding the flour into the mixture. Continue the folding action until the dough is smooth and not sticky. Adjust the amount of flour depending on how wet the dough is. Once you have formed the dough, knead it for 10 minutes, wrap it in plastic, and let it rest for at least 30 minutes.

continued.../

Doppio Ravioli with Fava Bean and Cheese Filling

Take the full amount of dough and cut it in half, keeping one half wrapped in plastic until you're done with the first half. Roll the dough flat with a rolling pin. Place the flattened dough into the pasta machine on the thickest setting and pass it through. Adjust the thickness of the setting with the knob, working toward thinner pasta. For filled-style pasta, I end with the third-lowest setting. Pass the pasta through the machine, and then fold the dough back up. Repeat the process 2 times. You might need to add a little flour if the pasta is sticking.

Folding and passing the dough through the pasta machine repeatedly builds structure into the pasta. Don't fold the pasta for the last pass through. You should have long sheets at this point. Cut the pasta sheet in half. Using your first pastry bag, pipe the cheese filling along the bottom of the first half pasta sheet. Run it along the whole length of the first half pasta sheet. Leave about a 1/2-inch space along the edge.

Using your second pastry bag, pipe the fava filling 1/8 inch from the cheese filling along the first half pasta sheet. Run it along the whole length of the first half pasta sheet, leaving about 1 or 2 inches at the ends. Then take a pastry brush or spray bottle of water and brush or spray the top and bottom portion with the fillings.

Take the second half pasta sheet and place it over the first half pasta sheet. You should now have two long tubes running all the way down the length of the pasta. At every 1/2 inch use a chopstick to press down to create the ends, and in-between both fillings to create doppio ravioli. Continue the same process all the way down the pasta sheet. Using a pinwheel cutter, cut away the excess pasta at the tops and bottoms of the raviolis. Cut in between each press that you make with the chopstick to create individual double raviolis. It should look something like the photo on page 99.

How to cook and finish ravioli

In a large sauté pan add 1 tablespoon of butter, 2 tablespoons of oil, and the maitake mushrooms. Cook for 3 minutes. Add the chili flakes and fava beans. Cook for another 1 minute, and then pour in the vegetable broth. Meanwhile, place your pasta into salted boiling water (2 tablespoons of salt, 12 cups of water) and cook for 2 to 3 minutes, or until the pasta floats to the top.

Strain off the water and place the pasta into the sauté pan. Let it simmer for 1 to 2 minutes, and then add the rest of the butter to make a pan sauce. Season the whole pan with salt. Place a few spoonfuls of pasta and mushrooms into each serving bowl. Finish with the chives, chive flowers, Parmesan cheese, and a drizzle of olive oil.

Note: Sometimes your ravioli isn't going to look perfect, but that doesn't affect the flavor! That is also a tell-tale sign that it is homemade, so don't stress over it! I don't!

Yin Yang Pasta with Lemon and Short Ribs (Summer and Winter)

SERVES 6–8

This recipe is a little yin and yang. It is two pasta dishes in one – lemon ricotta and braised beef au jus. My inspiration came from that moment when you're almost out of winter, but not quite into spring. You don't know whether you want something heavy or light. This dish has you covered!

Ingredients

Short ribs

3 pounds boneless Kobe short ribs, cut into 2-inch pieces
(If you have them on the bone, that is fine. There will be more flavor.)

3 tablespoons olive oil

1 onion

6 garlic cloves, chopped

2 carrots

2 stalks celery

3 cups red wine

3 tablespoons tomato paste

5 cups beef stock or chicken stock

1 sprig of rosemary

1 sprig of thyme, large

1 sprig of parsley, large

salt and pepper

Ricotta filling

1 pound fresh ricotta cheese

2 ounces grated Parmesan cheese

1 lemon, zested

salt and pepper

Instructions

For the short ribs

Season the short ribs with salt and pepper on both sides. In a medium-sized braising pot on high heat, add the oil and the short ribs. Sear for 5 minutes on the first side, and then turn the short ribs over. Add all the vegetables and cook for another 5 minutes. Add the wine and the tomato paste. Reduce the wine by half, and add your stock or water.

Bring to a boil, then turn down to a simmer. Add the herbs and cover. Cook for about 2 1/2 hours, or until the ribs are tender and almost falling apart. Take the meat out of the pot and place it into a bowl while it is still hot. Pour half of the liquid into a Vitamix, and add all the vegetables from the braising pot. Purée and pour over the short ribs. Let the meat rest in half of the purée liquid to cool completely. (The short ribs should be completely covered so as not to dry out.)

Place the other half of the braising liquid with the leftover purée sauce into a small saucepot and reduce it by half (or until it starts to thicken, or will glaze a spoon). Strain the sauce, and season with salt. Set aside, keeping it warm. When the short ribs have completely cooled, take them out of the purée sauce and chop or shred them somewhat fine. (You should almost be able to do this with your hands because the ribs will be so tender. You could do it in a food processor, but don't purée too much so you don't end up with baby food mashed meat!)

continued.../

Yin Yang Pasta with Lemon and Short Ribs
(Summer and Winter)

Agnolotti
2 cups flour

1 cup semolina

3 eggs

3 egg yolks

2 tablespoons warm water

1 teaspoon salt

Lemon sauce
1 cup cream

1 lemon, juiced

4 tablespoons butter

basil

Parmesan cheese

1 lemon, zested

Once you have a bowl of fine-shredded or chopped meat, season it with salt and pepper, and then add 8 ounces of the sauce to the meat to make it juicy but not runny. You want to make the meat taste delicious and moist. You don't want dried meat with no flavor for your agnolotti filling. Once you have a moist – not soaked – meat filling, place it back into the refrigerator until the sauce has adhered to the meat and congealed (about 2 hours).

For the ricotta filling

Place all the ingredients into a food processor. Purée everything until smooth. Season with salt and pepper. Place the filling into a plastic pastry bag, and then put it into the refrigerator for 30 minutes.

To make the agnolotti

Place the flour and semolina into a bowl. Make a well in the center of the flour. Add the eggs, egg yolks, water, and salt. With a fork, stir the egg mixture until it starts to form a ball of dough. Then use your hands to finish forming the dough. Add more flour if the dough is wet. Knead the pasta for 5 minutes, and then cover it and allow it to rest.

Cut your pasta in half. (Leave one half covered while you work with the other half.) Use a rolling pin to roll the dough so that it is thin enough to fit inside the thickest setting on your pasta machine.

Run the pasta all the way down to the lowest setting twice, dusting the dough with flour if it is too wet. Run it down a third time, but end with the second-lowest setting. Again, use a little flour for dusting. You should have long sheets at this point.

Using your pastry bag, pipe the cheese mixture along the bottom of the pasta, leaving about 1/2 inch from the edge clear. Also, run it along the whole length of the pasta sheet, leaving about 1 or 2 inches at the ends clear. (This looks like one long tube of filling. If you'd like to watch a tutorial about how to make agnolotti, go to www.saltandvanilla.com and click on *Video Recipes*.)

Yin Yang Pasta with Lemon and Short Ribs (Summer and Winter)

Using a pastry brush or spray bottle of water, brush or spray the top portion of the pasta sheet. Take the bottom part of the pasta closest to the filling and roll it over to the brushed-top portion. You should now have a long tube-like pasta running all the way down the length of the pasta sheet. Using your index fingers, press down at 1/2-inch intervals to create little "raviolis."

Continue the same process all the way down the pasta sheet. Next, using a pinwheel cutter, cut away the excess pasta at the top. Then cut in between each press that you made with your fingers to create each piece of your agnolotti. Place on a sheet pan lined with parchment paper and extra semolina flower to help prevent sticking. Set aside while you repeat the same process with the other half of the pasta ball.

This time you want to fill the pasta with the short rib filling, but instead of using a continuous line of filling, you should leave a gap of about 1/4 inch between each 1/2 inch covered with the short rib filling. This will create agnolotti the same size as the cheese-filled ones. Because the cheese filling is easy to manipulate, you can make one continuous line. On the other hand, the consistency of the meat allows you to leave a space between each piece of agnolotti. (The 1/4-inch space is where you will press your fingers to make the shape.) Continue this process along the whole length of the pasta and repeat the same steps from above with the cheese filling.

To finish

Place your beef agnolotti pasta in boiling salted water (2 tablespoons of salt, 12 cups of water) and cook for 2 to 3 minutes, or until they float to the top. Strain off the water and place the pasta into the sauté pan with the beef sauce. Add a touch of butter and season with salt and pepper. Set aside and keep warm.

Place your ricotta pasta into the water and cook for 2 to 3 minutes. Strain off the ricotta pasta and place it into a sauté pan with the cream, lemon juice, lemon zest, and 1/2 cup of the water used to cook the pasta. Let it simmer for 1 to 2 minutes, then add the rest of the butter to make a pan sauce. Season the whole pan with salt and pepper. Place 3 of each type of pasta into a bowl and garnish with basil and Parmesan cheese.

All Hands on Deck

The DeJorias planned a big gathering of friends and family for Easter Sunday. They arranged for a huge blow-up slide and a petting zoo for the kids. A sandy area had been designated for beach volleyball, and of course, lots of eggs were hidden for the traditional egg hunt. I planned a big spread for the whole day, featuring overnight-smoked beef ribs.

Who's Missing?

JP and Eloise couldn't be there for the party they'd organized. They were out of town and unfortunately unable to get back in time for the festivities. The DeJorias insisted that "the show must go on!" Everyone pitched in to help host the party, which speaks volumes about the trust that they extend to their staff and friends.

All in a Day's Work

It was a beautiful spring day and everyone enjoyed being outside, both in and out of the water. After cleanup I had the opportunity to pass the football around with an actor and some of the other guests. We ran routes in the backyard like we were pros. All in all it was a great day. I had prepared a Sunday spread, helped host a family party, and tossed the football around with an Academy Award winner. All right, all right, all right!

Beef Bolognese with Fettuccine

SERVES 6–8

Here's everyone's go-to pasta! Summertime screams tomatoes and basil for me. The sauces and soups you can make with these ingredients are endless. For this recipe, we are keeping everything simple—fresh fettuccine with tomato meat sauce. You can use whatever meat you desire. I like ground beef, veal, or a combination of the two.

Ingredients

Tomato sauce

5 tablespoons olive oil

1 onion, chopped

2 teaspoons chili flakes

4 garlic cloves, minced

4 cups fresh heirloom tomatoes or 2 boxes diced tomatoes

2 1/2 cups water

1 1/2 teaspoons salt

1/4 cup basil leaves

pepper

touch of cream, if desired

Basic egg pasta

(see page 313)

3 tablespoons olive oil

1/2 onion, diced

2 garlic cloves, minced

2 pounds Wagyu ground beef or veal

fennel seeds (optional)

3 ounces Parmesan cheese

1/4 cup basil leaves

salt and pepper

Instructions

How to make tomato sauce

The better the tomatoes, the better the sauce! This is my basic tomato sauce, but I have plenty of variations. In a saucepot, add 3 tablespoons of olive oil with the onion, chili flakes, and garlic. Cook for 3 minutes, then add the tomatoes. Add the water and 1 1/2 teaspoons of salt. Bring to a boil and cover with a lid. Cook for about 30 to 45 minutes, then add the basil leaves. With a hand blender or Vitamix, purée until smooth. Add salt and pepper, if needed. You may also add a touch of cream, if desired. Set aside and keep warm.

How to make fettuccine pasta

Make the *Basic Egg Pasta* dough described on page 313. Cut your pasta in half. (Leave one half covered while you work with the other half.) Use a rolling pin to roll the dough so that it is thin enough to fit inside the thickest setting on your pasta machine. Run the pasta all the way down to the lowest setting twice, dusting the dough with flour if it is too wet. Run it down a third time, ending on the third-lowest setting. Cut the pasta sheet at about 12 to 18 inches long.

Switch from the standard pasta attachment to the fettuccine attachment and feed the cut pasta sheets through it. The fettuccine should be long, flat, and ribbon-like. Dust them heavily with either semolina or flour so the noodles don't stick together.

continued.../

Beef Bolognese with Fettuccine

If you don't have the attachment, you can sprinkle the pasta sheet heavily with flour, and then roll the pasta up into a loose cigar shape. Cut the cigar every 1/4 inch. Once it is all cut up, you can gently fluff the pieces or unroll them to make your fettuccine. Place them onto a sheet pan lined with parchment paper, and then add more semolina or flour so the pasta doesn't stick. You can lay the fettuccine down in a circle pattern to make a "birds nest." Alternatively, you could hang the pasta to dry a bit.

How to cook and finish the pasta

In a large sauté pan, add the olive oil, onion, garlic, and beef. Season with salt and pepper. (Sometimes I like to add fennel seeds.) Cook for 10 minutes, and add 3 cups of tomato sauce. Cover and simmer for 5 minutes. Meanwhile, boil a pot of salted water (2 tablespoons of salt, 12 cups of water). Place 4 bundles (birds' nests) of fettuccine into the boiling water.

The fettuccine should cook for 1 to 2 minutes, or until it floats on top of the water and is tender. Strain out and place in the bolognese sauce along with a little pasta water, if the sauce is too thick. Toss well and adjust the seasoning, if need be. Then, taking a two-pronged roasting fork, twirl the pasta around the fork and place it into a bowl. Spoon a little extra meat sauce over the top. Grate fresh Parmesan cheese over the sauce, and then add basil leaves and a little drizzle of olive oil.

"Minestrone" White Bean Soup with Italian Chicken Sausage Ravioli

SERVES 6–8

When I came up with this recipe, my idea was to make a minestrone-type soup with pesto instead of tomato! I also wanted to celebrate the pasta more than the actual soup. I added spinach for the pasta dough to complement the color of the pesto. I decided to use chicken Italian sausage for the ravioli filling. The results were absolutely delicious!

Ingredients

White beans

1 pound white beans (soaked in water for at least 30 minutes, if possible)

1 onion, small-diced

3 cloves of garlic, minced

1 sprig of rosemary

12 cups water or chicken stock

2 teaspoons salt, plus more

Sausage

1 1/2 pounds ground chicken

5 cloves of garlic

1/2 onion

3 tablespoons parsley, chopped

1 tablespoon oregano

1 1/2 tablespoons fennel seeds

1/2 teaspoon chili flakes

1 tablespoon Italian seasoning

1 teaspoon olive oil

2 teaspoons salt

Sausage
(if you don't prepare your own)

1 1/2 pounds chicken Italian sausage, raw (remove the casing, if there is one)

Instructions

For the white beans

Drain the white beans and place them with all of the other listed ingredients into a soup pot. Place on top of the stove on medium-high heat. Bring to a boil, then turn down to a light simmer and cover. Cook for 30 minutes or so, and then add the salt. Continue to cook for another 25 to 30 minutes, or until the beans are just tender all the way through.

For the sausage (if you grind the meat yourself)

The most important step in making sausage is making sure your tools and meat are ice cold. (Some chefs place both the grinder attachments and bowl into the freezer to ensure this happens.) Fill a bowl with ice, and then set another bowl on top of the ice bowl. This will ensure that the meat will stay cold when it comes out of the grinder. Grind the chicken meat yourself (or have your local butcher grind it for you). Using the large die, run the meat, garlic, and onion through the meat grinder. Switching to the small die, run the chicken through the grinder a second time.

Add the rest of the ingredients to the chicken, then mix and season well. Place a small sauté pan on high heat with a teaspoon of olive oil. Cook 1/2 ounce of the chicken sausage mixture. Sample the sausage to see how it tastes. If everything is perfect, then set it aside for the pasta. If not, adjust the sausage, adding whatever you think it needs (salt, spice, etc.).

continued.../

"Minestrone" White Bean Soup with Italian Chicken Sausage Ravioli

Spinach Egg Pasta

3 cups flour

3 eggs, whole

3 egg yolks

2 tablespoons spinach purée

1 teaspoon salt

Garnish

1 yellow carrot,
sliced 1/8-inch thick

1 cup lima beans, frozen

1/3 cup pesto (see page 314)

4 teaspoons olive oil

3 ounces Parmesan cheese

How to make ravioli

Place the flour into a bowl. Make a well in the center of the flour. Add the eggs, egg yolks, spinach purée, and salt. With a fork, stir the egg mixture until it starts to form a ball of dough. Then use your hands to finish forming the dough. Add more flour if the dough is wet. Knead the pasta for 5 minutes, then cover it and allow it to rest for at least 30 minutes.

Cut your pasta in half. (Leave one half covered while you work with the other half.) Use a rolling pin to roll the dough so that it is thin enough to fit inside the thickest setting on your pasta machine. Run the pasta all the way down to the lowest setting twice, dusting the dough with flour if it is too wet. Run it down a third time, but end on the second-lowest setting. Again, use a little flour for dusting. You should have long sheets at this point. Cut the pasta sheet in half so you have two equal parts.

Using a pastry bag (or spoons), pipe a small amount of the chicken sausage mixture along the middle of one of the pasta sheets. Run it along the whole length of the pasta sheet, leaving about 1 inch between dollops of sausage filling. Use a pastry brush or spray bottle with water to brush or spray the top and bottom portions of the pasta sheet lightly.

Carefully place the second sheet of pasta on top. Using the back of a round cookie cutter or ring mold if you don't have a ravioli stamp or mold, shape the round ravioli around the filling, forcing any excess air out of your ravioli. (Air pockets will cause your pasta to explode in the water, so you want to avoid as much air inside the ravioli as possible.) To create a little ravioli, switch to a ring mold a few sizes bigger to cut the round ravioli.

Place the ravioli onto a sheet pan lined with parchment paper and extra semolina flour to help prevent sticking. Set aside while you repeat the same process with the other half of the pasta dough.

To finish

Put 8 cups of the bean-and-water mixture into a small pot to reheat it. Add carrot slices, lima beans, and pesto to the white beans, and season them with salt and pepper. Cook for 5 minutes. Bring another pot of salted water (2 tablespoons of salt, 12 cups of water) to a boil. Place half of the ravioli pasta into the pot, cooking it for 2 to 3 minutes. Strain out the pasta and place it into the pan with the bean pesto soup. Adjust the seasoning, if need be. Place a few spoonfuls of the ravioli and bean pesto soup into each serving bowl. Drizzle each serving with 1 teaspoon of olive oil and top with Parmesan cheese.

Surprise!

It was Super Bowl Sunday, and Tom Brady was going for his sixth ring later than night. I'd just been told that a European princess was coming to dinner with a few guests. This princess is also the coauthor of a cookbook and is passionate about food and cooking. Of course, a personal chef always wants to provide the best for any guests coming over, but when high profile guests are coming to dinner, I can't help but put additional pressure on myself.

Keeping things under wraps

What was really on my mind was a secret – I was flying my wife's family and best friend into town for her 40th birthday party. My wife had no idea that they were coming, and wouldn't, if I could only keep it together for a few more hours. So I kept to my normal schedule of shopping and running errands that day so nothing would seem out of the ordinary.

No time to spare

I was busy all morning doing those errands. I knew that both my boss and the princess should have been coming home around 3 or 4 p.m. The Super Bowl started around 5 p.m., and I knew they wanted to have some snacks around 4 p.m. By the time I had gone to a few different stores and gotten all the things I needed, it was close to 2 p.m. That meant I had very little time to come up with a creative dinner menu!

I wanted to make as many different dishes as possible, not just to give the guests variety, but also to use what I already had on hand. Thankfully, I had a co-worker to assist me. (The majority of the time I'm on my own.) I had no time to spare! It was time to get down to business! I fired up the pizza oven to roast Korean sweet potatoes and spiced Mediterranean carrots. I was also frying wonton cones for Kampachi poke and making charred onion guacamole, hummus, and crudités. Next came my version of tortellini en brodo (see page 115). Since I had plenty of Kampachi, I decided to sauté it with winter citrus to provide a nice contrast between raw and cooked fish.

My boss and the guests arrived right on time for dinner and everything went off without a hitch. They talked for a bit before deciding to sit down for dinner a little before 5 p.m. The princess was blown away by everything I made, which is always fantastic. She even went so far as to say to me that she had been in six different countries, including Italy and Greece, during the last six months and that this meal was the best she had eaten. Wow! What a compliment coming from someone who is well traveled and has eaten all over the world, not to mention the author of her own cookbook. I quickly took a photo with the princess, then sneaked out of the house to rush off to the airport.

Birthday surprise

I got to the airport a few minutes after my wife's sister and niece had landed. We drove back to our house and opened the door to my wife's complete shock. Later on I went to pick up her best friend for a fun-filled 40th birthday week. Seeing the joy on my wife's face as we walked through our front door made me thankful for the love of family and for our many blessings.

Tortellini en Brodo

SERVES 6-8

My version of this classic dish has no pork and also omits chicken in the broth. I use Wagyu beef for the tortellini filling and plate it in a smoked beef broth. Topped with fresh Parmesan cheese, this dish gives the original version some stiff competition.

Ingredients

Smoked bone broth

5 smoked beef rib bones

1 onion

1 leek

1 fennel

1 garlic bulb

12 cups water

2 celery ribs, chopped

2 carrots, chopped

salt

Meat tortellini filling

1 1/2 pounds Wagyu ground meat

1 egg

1 cup Parmesan cheese, finely-grated

1 tablespoon fennel seeds

4 cloves of garlic, grated

1 1/2 cups panko

4 tablespoons parsley, fresh-chopped

2 tablespoons oregano, fresh-chopped

2 tablespoons chive, fresh-chopped

1 tablespoon thyme, fresh-chopped

1 tablespoon salt

1 teaspoon red chili flakes

1 teaspoon black pepper

Instructions

How to make smoked bone broth

Place all the ingredients into a large stock pot and bring it to a boil. Turn down to a simmer and cook until you have about 5 cups left. Strain and season with salt. Set aside, and keep warm.

How to make the meat tortellini filling

This is my basic meatball recipe. Put all the ingredients into a stainless steel bowl, season, and mix well. In a small sauté pan, add 1 tablespoon of the meat mixture on high heat with a teaspoon of olive oil. Cook for 2 minutes, flip, and cook for 1 more minute. Taste the meat. If everything tastes perfect, then set the meat aside for the pasta. If not, add what you think the meat filling needs.

How to make tortellini pasta

Place 2 cups of flour and 1 cup of semolina into a bowl. Make a well in the center of the flour. Add the eggs, yolks, water, and salt. With a fork, stir the egg mixture until it starts to form a ball of dough. Then use your hands to finish forming the dough. Add more flour if the dough is wet. Knead the pasta for 5 minutes, and then cover it and allow it to rest for at least 30 minutes.

Cut your pasta in half. (Leave one half covered while you work with the other half.) Use a rolling pin to roll the dough so that it is thin enough to fit inside the thickest setting on your pasta machine.

Run the pasta all the way down to the lowest setting twice, dusting the dough with flour if it is too wet. Run it down a third time, ending on the third-lowest or fourth-lowest setting, depending on the strength of the dough. (If you believe the dough is very strong and has a good density to it, you might be fine with the third-lowest setting. If you believe the dough is "loose" and that it doesn't have a proper structure to it, then you might want to go a little thicker with the fourth-lowest setting.)

continued.../

Tortellini en Brodo

Tortellini pasta

2 cups flour

1 cup semolina

3 eggs

3 egg yolks

2 tablespoons warm water

1 teaspoon salt

Garnish

Parmesan cheese

chives

Once you have the flat pasta all laid out, you can use an adjustable pasta cutter to cut 1/2-inch by 1/2-inch squares. Add only a small amount of meatball filling to each pasta. Brush all of them with water. Fold each one into a triangle, and then pinch the ends together to make a tortellini shape. Place all of them onto a sheet pan lined with parchment paper.

To finish

Place a pot of salted water (2 tablespoons of salt, 12 cups of water) onto the stove and bring it to a boil. Place another pot on medium heat for the bone broth. Place 20 to 25 tortellini pastas into the water, allowing them to cook for 2 minutes. Strain them out and place them into the saucepan with the bone broth. Cook for another minute (until the tortellini is tender). Season with salt and pepper, if need be. Then portion the tortellini en brodo into 4 bowls. Top off with Parmesan cheese and chives.

Bucatini with
Eggplant Parmesan Sauce and Broccolini

SERVES 6–8

Here is a vegetarian-friendly pasta that is always a huge hit. I combine durum (semolina) and wheat flour for a little more "chew" in this recipe, but feel free to use the *Semolina Pasta* recipe at the end of the cookbook (page 313). I also toss in broccolini and spinach. Uncomplicated and delicious!

Ingredients

Eggplant Parmesan sauce

5 tablespoons olive oil

1 onion, chopped

2 teaspoons chili flakes

4 cloves of garlic, minced

4 cups fresh heirloom tomatoes

4 cups water

2 large eggplants, roasted

3 ounces fresh
Parmesan Reggiano cheese

1 Parmesan rind
(approximately 4 ounces)

1/4 cup basil leaves

salt and pepper

Tomato bucatini

3 cups semolina
(1 cup for dusting the noodles)

1 cup flour

1 1/4 cups warm water

2 tablespoons tomato paste

salt (optional)

Instructions

How to make eggplant Parmesan sauce

In a large saucepot, add the olive oil and the onions. Sauté for 4 minutes, then add the chili flakes and garlic. Cook for another 2 minutes, and add the tomatoes. Season the tomatoes with salt. (This will draw the water out of the tomatoes.) Add the water, roasted eggplant, 1/2 teaspoon of salt, and Parmesan rinds, and then bring to a boil. Turn down to a simmer and cover for 45 minutes. Then transfer everything but the Parmesan rinds into a Vitamix, adding the basil leaves and the Parmesan cheese. (You might have to blend in batches.) Season with salt and pepper.

How to make tomato bucatini

Place 2 cups of semolina and 1 cup of flour into a bowl. Make a well in the center of the flour. Add the water, tomato paste, and salt. With a fork stir the mixture until it starts to form a ball of dough. Then use your hands to finish forming the dough. Add more flour if the dough is wet. Knead the pasta for 10 minutes, and then cover it and allow it to rest for at least 30 minutes. Cut the dough into manageable pieces and place them into a pasta extruder.

The bucatini should be about 10 to 12 inches long, so you will need to cut them when the noodles reach that length. Place them onto a sheet pan lined with parchment paper and semolina flour. Dust the pasta on the pan heavily with semolina so the pasta doesn't stick. Continue the process until all the dough is extruded.

continued.../

Bucatini with Eggplant Parmesan Sauce and Broccolini

2 tablespoons olive oil

1 tablespoon butter

8 ounces broccolini

1 clove of garlic, minced

1 pound spinach

1/2 teaspoon chili flakes

2 ounces Parmesan cheese

1 drizzle olive oil

1/4 cup basil leaves

salt

To finish

In a large sauté pan, add 2 tablespoons of olive oil, 1 tablespoon of butter, and 8 ounces of broccolini. Cook for 2 minutes, then add a pinch of salt. Add the garlic and the spinach to the pan and cook for another 2 minutes. Place your bucatini pasta into boiling salted water (2 tablespoons of salt, 12 cups of water) and cook for 3 to 4 minutes (until the bucatini floats to the top). Strain out and place into the pan with the vegetables. Add the eggplant Parmesan sauce to the noodles. Season everything with salt. Then add the pasta to each serving plate with some of the vegetables and sauce. Top with chili flakes and shaved Parmesan cheese. Drizzle everything with a little olive oil, and add some basil leaves.

Culurgiones

SERVES 6-8

Here is the signature pasta dish of Sicily. In southern Italy a semolina-style pasta dough is more common than the northern-style made with eggs. Feel free to substitute whichever dough you prefer, but for this recipe, I chose the semolina-style pasta.

Ingredients

Culurgiones filling

1 russet potato, boiled and mashed

2 ounces mozzarella cheese

2 to 3 ounces Parmesan cheese

2 to 3 ounces Manchego cheese

2 tablespoons tarragon, chopped

2 tablespoons chives, chopped

3 to 4 tablespoons butter

3 tablespoons crème fraîche

salt and pepper

Basil pesto sauce

(see page 314)

Culurgiones pasta

3 cups semolina

1 1/4 cups warm water

salt (optional)

Charred tomato butter

(see page 313)

Instructions

How to make culurgiones filling

Place all the ingredients into a bowl and mix well. Season with salt and pepper. Allow to cool to room temperature.

How to make culurgiones pasta

Place the semolina flour into a bowl. Make a well in the center of the flour. Add the water and mix with your hands until you make a dough. Knead the dough for 10 minutes (or until it is smooth), and then wrap it and allow it to rest.

Using a bench scraper or knife, cut the dough in half. Pass your dough through the pasta machine and work it down to the second-to-last setting. Repeat the process.

Next, use a 3 1/2-inch ring mold to cut out circles. Place your culurgiones filling into the center of each pasta round. You want to overstuff the round. Then fold the pasta into a "taco" shape around the filling. Alternate your thumb and index finger as you fold, then pinch the sides together. As you are folding the seam, you should be pushing the excess filling out of the pasta round. Continue this step until the pasta is sealed tightly. The seal on the pasta should look like a zipper. Continue until you have no more filling.

To finish

Place a pot of salted water (2 tablespoons of salt, 12 cups of water) onto the stove and bring it to a boil. Place the culurgiones into the water and boil them for 2 to 3 minutes. Strain them out and place them into two different pans. Place 1/4 cup of the pesto sauce into one sauté pan with 1/3 cup of the pasta water, and place 1 1/2 cups of tomato butter into the other pan. Season with salt and pepper, and then place a portion of each into every serving bowl. Shave a few pieces of Parmesan cheese on top.

Mafaldine Pasta with Red Snapper, Parsley, and Lemon Butter

SERVES 6–8

This recipe was inspired by a dish I once had in Milan. It was so simple in concept. The rich, deep flavor of the fish stock is the building block of this dish. The two sauces add a really fresh look and taste. This recipe requires a bit more time to make, but it is well worth the time and effort.

Ingredients

Fish stock

1 carcass snapper, including scraps and skin

1 carrot

1 onion

1 leek

3 stalks celery

1 garlic bulb, cut in half

1 bay leaf

3 sprigs of thyme

1 tablespoon black peppercorns

10 cups water

Parsley sauce

3 cups fish stock

1 to 2 bunches of parsley, blanched

2 tablespoons butter

salt

Beurre blanc sauce

1 cup white wine

1/2 teaspoon zest

1 sprig of thyme

1 clove of garlic

1 cup cream

1 to 1 1/2 sticks butter

1 lemon, juiced

salt

Instructions

For the fish stock

Have your butcher fillet the snapper if you cannot do it yourself. Reserve the fillets for the pasta. Cut the collar off the fish and reserve it for another use. Take the gills out and discard them. Rinse the fish carcass well under cold water to remove any blood, which will turn your stock cloudy. Place the carcass into a pot with the rest of the ingredients, except the parsley, butter, and salt. Bring it to a boil.

Turn down to a simmer and reduce by at least half. The stock should have a deep, rich flavor. If the stock still tastes very mild and watery, then reduce it a little more until you have a deep flavor profile. Strain out and discard the contents.

For the parsley sauce

To turn the stock into a parsley sauce, put 3 cups of the fish stock into a blender with the blanched parsley. Purée until smooth, add a little butter, and season with salt. Set aside and keep warm

For the beurre blanc sauce

In a small saucepot add the white wine, zest, thyme, and garlic. Reduce the liquid until the wine is just about evaporated (about 3/4 reduced). Add the cream and reduce that by half. Finish by adding the butter to the sauce 1 tablespoon at a time, waiting for it to emulsify. Season with salt, add lemon juice, and strain, if desired. Set aside and keep warm.

continued.../

Mafaldine Pasta with Red Snapper, Parsley, and Lemon Butter

Pasta

10 ounces Mafaldine pasta
(store-bought), cooked al dente

Snapper

1 pound snapper, large-diced,
skin removed

salt and pepper

Garnish

Parmesan cheese

parsley sprigs

To finish

Bring a pot of salted water (2 tablespoons of salt, 12 cups of water) to a boil. Place the Mafaldine pasta into the pot, cooking it until it is al dente (approximately 10 minutes). Meanwhile, in a large sauté pan, add 2 cups of parsley sauce. Season the diced snapper with salt and place it into the sauce. Put the sauté pan on medium heat.

Cook the snapper gently in the sauce until it is just done. It should take only 1 or 2 minutes. Toss in the strained-out pasta and cook for another 1 or 2 minutes so the pasta soaks up the sauce. Season everything with salt and pepper.

Place a few spoonfuls of the beurre blanc sauce into the bottom of each serving bowl. Place the snapper Mafaldine pasta on top. Use a hand blender to froth the leftover parsley sauce. Spoon the froth over the pasta. Finish with Parmesan cheese and parsley sprigs.

Carnival Squash Scarpinocc with Sunchoke

SERVES 6–8

To celebrate the many different squashes available in the winter months, I've made a soup with butternut squash and a pasta filling with carnival squash. I chose Scarpinocc, a shoe-shaped pasta, that is fun to make but a bit time-consuming. The combination of soup, pasta, and fried sunchoke chips is perfect on a chilly winter night!

Ingredients

Carnival squash filling

1 1/2 cups carnival squash, roasted
1 pound ricotta cheese
2 ounces Parmesan cheese
1 tablespoon basil, chopped
salt and pepper

Scarpinocc pasta

(see page 313)

Butternut squash soup

2 tablespoons butter
1/2 onion, sliced thin
3 cloves of garlic, roasted
1 small butternut squash, roasted
4 to 5 cups chicken broth
salt and pepper

Roasted sunchokes

12 ounces sunchokes
3 tablespoons olive oil
salt and pepper

Fried sunchokes

3 large sunchokes, shaved thin
1 1/2 cups vegetable oil
salt

2 tablespoons olive oil

Instructions

How to make the carnival squash filling

Cut the carnival squash in half, scoop out the seeds, and place the squash onto a sheet pan lined with parchment paper. Drizzle 1 tablespoon of olive oil in each half. Season with salt, and flip over so the squash is face down. Place in an oven at 400 degrees for 45 to 50 minutes, or until the squash is tender all the way through. Remove from the oven and allow it to cool completely.

Put the roasted carnival squash, ricotta, Parmesan cheese, basil, salt, and pepper into a food processor. Purée until the mixture is completely smooth, then place it into a pastry bag with a plain tip. Put it into the refrigerator for 30 minutes to firm the filling slightly.

How to make scarpinocc pasta

Begin by making the dough according to the recipe for *Basic Egg Pasta* on page 313. Cut your pasta in half. (Leave one half covered while you work with the other half.) Use a rolling pin to roll the dough so that it is thin enough to fit inside the thickest setting on your pasta machine. Run the pasta all the way down to the lowest setting twice, dusting the dough with flour if it is too wet. Run it down a third time, ending with the second-lowest or third-lowest setting, depending on the strength of the dough. Again, use a little flour for dusting. (If you believe the dough is very strong and has a good density to it, you might be fine with the second-lowest setting. If you believe that the dough is "loose" and that it doesn't have a proper structure to it, then you might want to go a little thicker, ending with the third-lowest setting.)

continued.../

Carnival Squash Scarponicc with Sunchoke

2 tablespoons butter
2 ounces Parmesan cheese, grated
3 tablespoons pumpkin seed oil
3 tablespoons chives, chopped
salt and pepper

Once you have the flat pasta all laid out, you can use an adjustable pasta cutter to cut 1-inch by 1/2-inch rectangles. Place a dollop of filling into the center of each rectangle pasta. Fold the pasta once over the filling and then once more to seal it. Pinch both sides of the rectangle, and then using your finger, make a little dimple in the top of your filling.

How to make butternut squash soup

In a small saucepot add the butter and onion slices with a pinch of salt. Cook for a few minutes, and then add the roasted garlic and the roasted butternut squash. Add the chicken broth and bring to a boil. Turn down to a simmer and cook for 15 minutes. Place into a Vitamix and purée until smooth. Season with salt and pepper, and keep warm.

How to roast sunchokes

Wash and dry the sunchokes, then place them onto a sheet pan lined with parchment paper. Drizzle with olive oil and season with salt and pepper. Put the sheet pan into an oven preheated to 375 degrees and roast the sunchokes for 30 minutes, moving them around the pan periodically during the cooking process. Take the sunchokes out of the oven and let them cool completely. Once they have cooled, slice them for use in finishing the pasta.

How to fry sunchokes

Slice the sunchokes thin. In a small pot, add the vegetable oil for frying and bring the heat to 315 degrees. Add the sunchokes in small batches, making sure not to add too many, which would overcrowd the pan. Fry until they are crisp. Strain out and season immediately with salt.

To finish

Boil a pot of salted water (2 tablespoons of salt, 12 cups of water). In a large sauté pan, add 2 tablespoons each of olive oil and butter. Add the sliced, roasted sunchokes into the pan. Place the scarpinocc pasta into the boiling water and cook for 2 minutes. Then strain the pasta out and place it into the sauté pan with the sunchokes. Season with salt and pepper.

To serve, pour some of the butternut squash soup into each bowl. Add a few pieces of the pasta with the sunchokes. Top with some fresh Parmesan cheese. Drizzle with pumpkin seed oil. Top with sunchoke chips and chives.

Parsnip Tortellini with Foie Gras and Celery

SERVES 6–8

More inspiration from Italy prompted this recipe. The parsnip filling and foie gras sauce make this pasta dish unconventional, but phenomenal. The addition of aged balsamic vinegar offsets the richness. Fried parsnips coat the pasta for crunch. Celery leaves and Parmesan cheese round out the dish.

Ingredients

Parsnip filling

2 tablespoons olive oil

2 tablespoons butter

3 to 4 large parsnips, peeled and sliced

2 tablespoons cream (if need be)

8 ounces mascarpone cheese

2 ounces Parmesan cheese

1/2 teaspoon salt

pepper

Tortellini

3 eggs

3 egg yolks

2 3/4 cups flour

1 teaspoon salt

splash of water

Fried parsnips

3 parsnips, chopped

1 cup water

2 cups vegetable oil

Instructions

How to make parsnip filling

In a medium saucepan add the oil, butter, and parsnips, with a fair amount of salt distributed evenly on the parsnips. Use medium-low heat to prevent coloring the parsnips. Place a lid on top and shake the pot every other minute to move the vegetables around. The salt will leach the water out of the vegetables and they will cook in their own juices. Cook for 20 minutes, and then check the vegetables. Cook for another 10 minutes (until they are tender), and then place them into a food processor or Vitamix with a touch of cream, and the mascarpone cheese, Parmesan cheese, salt, and pepper. Purée until silky smooth.

How to make tortellini

After making your pasta dough (see *Basic Egg Pasta* on page 313), cut your pasta in half. (Leave one half covered while you work with the other half.) Use a rolling pin to roll the dough so that it is thin enough to fit inside the thickest setting on your pasta machine.

Run the pasta all the way down to the lowest setting twice, dusting the dough with flour if it is too wet. Run it down a third time, but end with the third-lowest or second-lowest setting, depending on the strength of the dough. Again, use a little flour for dusting. (If you believe that the dough is very strong and has a good density to it, you might be fine with the second-lowest setting. If you believe that the dough is "loose" and that it doesn't have a proper structure to it, then you might want to go a little thicker, ending with the third-lowest setting.)

Foie gras sauce

3 cups smoked beef stock

12 ounces foie gras

4 tablespoons butter

sherry vinegar

salt and pepper

Garnish

1 ounce Parmesan cheese

1/2 cup celery leaves (from the heart)

1 small bottle best, aged, thick balsamic vinegar (Mussini Delizia 30 Year Balsamic Vinegar or Gourmet Blends balsamic vinegar)

Once you have the flat pasta all laid out, you can use an adjustable pasta cutter to cut 1/2-inch by 1/2-inch squares. Use only a small amount of filling for each pasta, and then brush the pasta with water. Fold each over into a triangle, and then pinch the ends together to make a tortellini shape. Place them onto a sheet pan lined with parchment paper.

Fried parsnips

Meanwhile, in a food processor, place 3 chopped parsnips and 1 cup of water. Purée them until all the parsnips are small pieces (think brunoise or small dice) and are about the same size. Strain out the water from the parsnips, and using paper towels, dry them as much as possible. In a small pot with 2 cups of vegetable oil at 325 degrees, fry the parsnips in batches until golden brown. Strain out and season with salt.

How to make foie gras sauce

Place the 3 cups of beef stock into a pot and reduce down to 1 1/2 cups. Then place a sauté pan on high heat. Season the foie gras with salt and pepper, and cook on both sides for 2 minutes. Pour the beef stock into a Vitamix together with the cooked foie gras and fat that is in the pan. Purée until smooth, and then add the butter and sherry vinegar. Season with salt. Set aside and keep warm.

To finish

Place 20 tortellini into boiling salted water (2 tablespoons of salt, 12 cups of water) and cook for 2 to 3 minutes. Strain out and place into the sauté pan with a little pasta water and foie gras sauce. Cook for 1 minute. Add salt and pepper, if need be. Then portion the tortellini into 4 bowls. Top off with Parmesan cheese, fried parsnips, and celery leaves. Drizzle with balsamic vinegar.

Pici Cacio e Pepe

SERVES 6-8

A trip to Tuscany provided my inspiration for this recipe. I had never had pici pasta before spending a week in Cortona, Italy. This pasta is the original "mac-and-cheese" recipe of Italy. The magic of this dish is all in the execution. Toasting the pepper, melting the cheese properly, and tossing the pasta continually (so the sauce adheres to the pasta), is what makes a perfect cacio e pepe.

Ingredients

Semolina pasta

2 cups semolina

1 cup flour

1 1/4 cups warm water

salt (optional)

Sauce

1 to 2 teaspoons pepper, fresh-cracked

4 tablespoons butter

3/4 cup pasta water (reserved from cooking the pasta)

4 ounces Pecorino Romano cheese, finely grated

salt

Instructions

For the pasta

Place both flours into a bowl. Make a well in the center of the flour, and add the warm water. Then use your hands to form a dough. Knead the dough for 10 minutes (until it is smooth), and then wrap it and allow it to rest for 30 minutes.

Using a bench scraper or a knife, cut the dough in half. Cut the dough into 5 equal slices, then cut those slices in half again, so you should have 10 small pieces of dough about 1 inch in length. With your hands, start rolling the pieces into long ropes. You don't want to stretch the dough, but the pressure from your hands should lengthen the pici pasta.

Continue rolling until you have long noodles that are a touch bigger than spaghetti. (You might want to cut them in half if they are too long.) Place the noodles onto a sheet pan lined with parchment paper and lots of semolina flour. Try not to add a lot of flour when you're rolling out the pici. (This might dry out your dough, causing it to crack.)

To finish

Fill a large pot with salted water (2 tablespoons of salt, 12 cups of water) and bring it to a boil. Add the pasta to the water and cook for 3 to 5 minutes, or until the pasta is tender. Meanwhile, in a large sauté pan, add fresh cracked pepper, toasting it for 30 seconds. Then add 4 tablespoons of butter to the pan and allow it to melt, but not to brown. Add 3/4 cup of the pasta water to the pan to emulsify the sauce. Drain the pasta and add it to the pan. Toss the pasta in the sauce for 1 minute. Take the pan off the heat, and then add the finely grated Pecorino Romano cheese. Stir continuously for at least 1 minute so that the cheese blends with the pasta, butter, and water to create a creamy sauce. If it looks dry, add a touch of pasta water. If it is a bit loose, continue stirring and add a touch more cheese. Garnish with black pepper and more cheese.

Cheese Agnolotti with Cherries and Balsamic Vinegar

SERVES 6–8

This recipe honors the versatility of pasta and the fusion of summer ingredients. Cheese, cherries, balsamic vinegar, and pasta describe this dish in a nutshell. The combination offers the unexpected flavor that makes this pasta unique and addictive.

Ingredients

Cheese filling
1 pound ricotta cheese
4 ounces P'tite Basque Cheese
2 ounces Parmesan cheese
1/2 teaspoon salt
1/2 teaspoon pepper

Agnolotti pasta
3 cups flour
3 whole eggs
3 egg yolks
2 tablespoons warm water
1 teaspoon salt

1 stick butter
1 cup cherries, halved and pitted
2 ounces aged balsamic vinegar (or glaze)
salt and pepper

Garnish
1 handful basil leaves

Instructions

For the cheese filling
Place all of the ingredients into a food processor and purée until smooth. Season with salt and pepper, and place into a plastic pastry bag.

How to make agnolotti pasta
Place 3 cups of flour into a bowl. Make a well in the center of the flour. Add the eggs, egg yolks, water, and salt. With a fork stir the egg mixture until it starts to form a ball of dough. Then use your hands to finish forming the dough. Add more flour if the dough is wet. Knead the pasta for 5 minutes, then cover it and allow it to rest for at least 30 minutes.

Cut your pasta in half. (Leave one half covered while you work with the other half.) Use a rolling pin to roll the dough so that it is thin enough to fit inside the thickest setting on your pasta machine.

Run the pasta all the way down to the lowest setting twice, dusting the dough with flour if it is too moist. Run it down a third time, but end with the second-lowest setting. Again, use a little flour for dusting. You should have long sheets at this point.

Using your pastry bag, pipe the cheese mixture along the bottom of the pasta, leaving about 1/2 inch from the edge clear. Run the mixture along the whole length of the pasta sheet, leaving about 1 or 2 inches at the ends clear. This should make one long tube of filling.

continued.../

Cheese Agnolotti with Cherries and Balsamic Vinegar

Using a pastry brush or spray bottle of water, brush or spray the top portion of the pasta sheet. Roll the bottom part of the pasta over the filling, sealing it to the top portion. You should now have a long tube-like pasta running all the way down the length of the pasta sheet. Using your index fingers, press down at 1/2-inch intervals to create little "raviolis."

Continue the same process all the way down the pasta sheet. Next, using a pinwheel cutter, cut away the excess pasta at the top. Then cut between each press that you made with your fingers to create each piece of agnolotti. Place on a sheet pan lined with parchment paper and extra semolina flower to help prevent sticking. Set aside while you repeat the same process with the other half of the pasta ball.

To finish

Place your pasta into boiling salted water (2 tablespoons of salt, 12 cups of water) and cook for 2 to 3 minutes, or until it floats to the top. Strain off and place the pasta into the sauté pan with 1/2 cup of the cooking water, along with the butter, to make a pan sauce. Season the whole pan with salt and pepper.

In a separate pan, add the cherries and cook on medium heat for 2 minutes. Then add 1 ounce of balsamic vinegar to the pan, cooking for another 3 to 4 minutes. Turn off the heat, then place about 5 agnolotti onto each plate with some of the butter sauce. Add some cherries to the pasta. Drizzle the whole plate with a little more aged balsamic vinegar (or glaze), and then finish with a few leaves of basil.

Black Truffle Cavatelli and Fondue

SERVES 6–8

Indulgence is the word for this pasta dish. This recipe may seem a little over-the-top with the addition of the fondue cheese foam, but these lush flavors are melt-in-your-mouth delicious!

Ingredients

Cavatelli pasta

2 cups semolina

1 cup flour

1 1/4 cups warm water

salt

Fondue

3 tablespoons butter

3 tablespoons flour

3 to 3 1/2 cups milk

2 ounces shredded fontina cheese

1 ounce shredded Parmesan cheese

2 ounces shredded truffle cheese

salt

3/4 cup pasta water

2 ounces Parmesan cheese, finely grated

1 stick butter or truffle butter

1 teaspoon black truffle oil

1 fresh black truffle

salt and pepper

Instructions

How to make cavatelli pasta

Place 2 cups of semolina and 1 cup of flour into a bowl and mix them well. Make a well in the center of the flour. Add the water and salt. With a fork stir the mixture until it starts to form a ball of dough. Then use your hands to finish forming the dough. Add more flour if the dough is wet. Knead the pasta for 10 minutes, and then cover it and allow it to rest for at least 30 minutes.

After the dough has rested, use a bench scraper or knife to cut the dough in half, then cut each half into 5 equal slices. Using your hands, roll the slices into a rope. Cut the ropes into dime-sized pieces that are round. Using a paring knife or your index finger and middle finger, press the little pieces of pasta, curling them toward you. Place the pasta onto a sheet pan lined with parchment paper and a dusting of semolina flour.

How to make fondue

In a saucepot on medium heat, add the butter. After the butter has melted, add the flour to make a roux. Once the roux has formed, add the milk one cup at a time, stirring continually with a whisk. Keep adding the milk until a thick sauce has formed.

Place on medium-low heat for 5 to 7 minutes to cook out the flour. Add the cheese and melt it completely. Finish the fondue with salt. Once it has been seasoned and has melted all together, pour it into an iSi canister and charge with 1 to 2 cartridges. (This step is completely optional. It incorporates air into the fondue, which will transform it into a melt-in-your-mouth foam.) Keep the canister in a hot water bath to ensure the fondue will remain hot.

continued.../

Black Truffle Cavatelli and Fondue

How to cook pasta and finish the dish

Fill a large pot with salted water (2 tablespoons of salt, 12 cups of water) and bring to boil. Add the pasta to the water and cook for 3 to 5 minutes (until tender). Drain the pasta, but reserve 3/4 cup of the water.

Meanwhile, in a large sauté pan add the reserved pasta water, the finely grated Parmesan cheese, and the butter. Swirl the pan around so that the butter and cheese start to melt and take on a sauce-like consistency (1 minute). Add the drained pasta, and then toss to coat the pasta well. Season with salt, black pepper, and truffle oil. Place the cavatelli onto each plate. Using the iSi canister, foam the fondue next to the pasta. Finish with truffles..

Fish is an excellent source of protein and one that can be prepared quickly. The different textures and flavors have a lot to do with the oils and fat content in fish. A very lean fish, without a lot of fat or oil, tends to be dry when slightly overcooked (think halibut). Fish with a lot of fat and oil, like sea bass or black cod, stay moist and juicy. Keep this distinction in mind as you are preparing these recipes. The difference between undercooked, properly cooked, and overcooked can be seconds, in some cases.

I enjoy cooking fish, but I am concerned about the devastating effects of global overfishing. For that reason, my recipes call for fish harvested in a sustainable way or farmed responsibly. The Monterey Bay Aquarium Seafood Watch can give you an up-to-date, comprehensive guide that includes a list of sustainable seafood. If you want to know more about where the best fish for eating are, check out the app.

Choosing fish at a supermarket or from a fishmonger can be challenging. Here are some tips to ensure you are choosing the freshest catch: 1) find out when the market receives its fish orders and plan to shop on those days; 2) when buying a whole fish, look for clarity in the eyes – that means no cloudiness; 3) ask to look behind the gills – they should be bright red and not brownish or slimy; 4) check out the firmness of the fish by poking one finger into the body; if the fish does not bounce back, it is old; 5) when buying fillets, look at color and appearance; and 6) fresh fish should smell like the water where it was caught – it should never smell fishy.

I hope the diversity of recipes in this chapter gives you confidence working with fish!

FISH

Red Snapper Escabeche

SERVES 8

This is my interpretation of a classic Spanish dish typically consisting of marinated fish, meat, or vegetables cooked in a vinegar base. The addition of capers, dill, and jalapeño peppers really gives the dish an extra punch! This presentation is playful (serving the fish in a sardine can) and really creates a splash!

Ingredients

1 pound red snapper, sliced thin (nigiri style)

Escabeche
1/4 cup white wine vinegar
1/4 cup sherry vinegar
1/4 cup apple cider vinegar
1/4 cup rice wine vinegar
1/4 cup capers and some of the juice
1 to 2 tablespoons salt
3 shallots or 1/2 red onion, brunoise-cut
2 jalapeño peppers, brunoise-cut
1 red bell pepper, brunoise-cut
1 yellow bell pepper, brunoise-cut
1 orange bell pepper, brunoise-cut
1 clove of garlic, minced
1 cup olive oil
2 tablespoons dill, chopped

Garnish
microgreens
dill

Instructions

How to make escabeche

In a small pot add all the vinegars and 1 tablespoon of salt. Bring to a boil. Meanwhile, place all the capers, vegetables, and garlic into a heat-proof bowl. Once the vinegar comes to a boil and the salt is dissolved, pour the vinegar over all the vegetables. Let the contents cool for at least 10 minutes. Add the oil and probably another 1 or 2 teaspoons of salt. Let the bowl cool completely, and then add the juice from the capers and the chopped dill. Check to see whether you need to adjust the seasoning.

To finish

For this appetizer, I emptied cans of store-bought sardines, washed the cans, and used them as my plates. Place 4 to 5 pieces of snapper into the bottoms of each tin. Season them with salt. Spoon the escabeche all over the fish. Top with micro greens and dill.

Note: The longer you leave the escabeche on the fish, the more the vinegars change the texture. This is not a bad thing. Let the fish sit about 3 to 5 minutes before you serve it. Time allows the flavors to marinate together. (You can wait as long as an hour, if you would like.)

Petrale Sole with Pea Purée, Kimchi, and Brown Butter Sauce

SERVES 4

In this recipe I combine Asian flavors with California grapes and tomatoes. The dish is perfect for any clean-eating summer meal. It really checks all the boxes with flavor, simplicity, and umami.

Ingredients

Pea purée
1 1/2 cups peas
1 teaspoon koji
2 teaspoons yellow miso
1/8 cup cream, warmed
1 tablespoon butter
1/4 cup cilantro leaves

Petrale sole
4 fillets petrale sole
4 teaspoons kimchi paste (homemade or store-bought)
2 tablespoons olive oil
1 cup Thomcord grapes
1 cup cherry tomatoes, red and orange
1 stick butter
3 tablespoons soy sauce
salt

Garnish
micro cilantro

Instructions

How to make pea purée

Place a small pot of salted water (1 tablespoon of salt, 4 cups of water) on high heat and bring to a boil. Once the water boils, place the peas into the water and cook for 2 to 3 minutes, or until they just get tender all the way through.

Then strain out the peas and place them into a blender with the rest of the ingredients. Purée all the ingredients until smooth. Adjust seasoning, if needed, with a pinch of salt. (Add lime, if you want.) Set aside and keep warm.

How to cook petrale sole

Season the sole with salt on both sides of the fish. Then spread a teaspoon of kimchi paste evenly onto the top of each fillet of sole. In a pan on medium-high heat, add 2 tablespoons of olive oil. Place the sole face down (with the kimchi) into the pan. Cook for 3 minutes, or until golden brown.

About 2 minutes into cooking the fish, add your grapes and tomatoes to the pan. Flip the fish over and cook for 1 more minute. Then take the fish out and place onto 4 different plates. Add the butter, melting it until the butter starts to brown all the way through. Add the soy sauce and season, if need be. Then spoon the sauce, grapes, and tomatoes over the top of the sole. Add the pea purée next to the fish. Garnish with micro cilantro.

Fish and Chips

SERVES 4

Fish wrapped in chips? This dish was inspired by an appetizer I made years ago at a restaurant that served a similar dish with scallops. I added a twist by wrapping the fish in shoestring potatoes and making an Asian "tartar" sauce to compliment it!

Ingredients

Asian gribiche
6 hard-boiled egg yolks
1 habanero pepper
1 garlic clove
3 tablespoons tamari
3 tablespoons koji
1/4 cup pickle juice
2 tablespoons rice wine vinegar
2 tablespoons Dijon mustard
1/2 cup oil
salt

Tempura
1/4 cup flour
1/2 cup rice four
1/2 cup corn starch
3/4 cup to 1 cup cold soda water
1 1/2 potatoes, peeled, julienned, and blanched
1 pound cod or black cod, cut into 6 pieces of about 2 1/2 ounces each
salt

Garnish
fried celery leaves
chives
horseradish, grated

Instructions

How to make gribiche
Place the hard-boiled egg yolks, habanero pepper, garlic, tamari, koji, pickle juice, vinegar, and mustard into a blender. Purée until smooth. While running the blender, add the oil in a smooth, slow, steady stream until the sauce emulsifies. Season with salt. Set aside for later.

How to prepare tempura fish
Place your flour, rice flour, and cornstarch into a bowl. Season lightly with salt, and then pour into the soda water. Stir together with a whisk until the mixture resembles a light batter. Drain a handful of julienne potatoes well, and then place them into the tempura batter. Place 1 piece of fish into the middle and wrap the potato and batter all around the fish.

To finish
Place the fish into a fryer at 350 degrees and fry for 4 to 5 minutes (until golden brown and cooked through). Take the fish out and place it onto a paper towel to drain. Season with salt. Repeat with the remaining pieces of fish. Place a spoonful of the gribiche sauce onto each plate. Place the fish and chips on top. Finish with fried celery leaves, chives, and freshly grated horseradish.

Mahi-Mahi with Sourdough, Cabbage, and Roasted Garlic

SERVES 4

Mahi-mahi is a tasty fish that is typically wild-caught, and it remains juicy after being cooked. This budget-friendly dish can be prepared in 30 minutes, assuming you already have the garlic prepared. I crusted the fish with a piece of sourdough bread and served it with cabbage, black-eyed peas, and a roasted garlic sauce.

Ingredients

Cabbage
2 tablespoons butter
2 tablespoons oil
1/2 cabbage
1 teaspoon salt

Black-eyed peas
2 cups fresh black-eyed peas
6 cups water
1 sprig of thyme
2 cloves of garlic
1 1/2 teaspoons salt

Roasted garlic aioli
1/2 cup roasted garlic
1 cup Vegenaise
1/2 teaspoon salt

Mahi-mahi
1 1/2 pounds mahi-mahi, cut into 6-ounce pieces
4 tablespoons harissa paste
4 slices sourdough bread
salt

3 tablespoons olive oil
2 tablespoons butter
chives

Instructions

For the cabbage
Add the butter, oil, and cabbage to a braising pan heated to medium. Add the salt to the cabbage in layers so that all the ingredients get a little salt. (Adding salt and covering the pot sweats the vegetables. Salt draws water out of the vegetables so they cook in their own liquid.) Keep an eye on maintaining medium heat so the vegetables don't burn. After a 25-minute sweat, the cabbage should be tender and melt in your mouth.

For the black-eyed peas
Fresh black-eyed peas will always take about half the amount of time as dried. Place all the ingredients into a pot and bring it to a boil, then turn down the heat and simmer for about 20 to 25 minutes, or until the black-eyed peas are cooked through. Adjust the seasoning, if need be.

For the roasted garlic aioli
Place the roasted garlic and Vegenaise into a Vitamix and purée until smooth. Season with salt and set aside.

For the mahi-mahi
Season 4 pieces of mahi-mahi with salt. Using an offset spatula, spread 1 tablespoon of harissa paste onto each piece of fish on the fillet side. Place a slice of sourdough bread on top of each fish. Flip them all over so the bread is down on the cutting board. Trim the edges of the bread slices so they are just about the same size as the fish fillets.

To finish

In a sauté pan on medium heat, add the olive oil and butter. Place the fish bread-side down and cook it for about 4 to 5 minutes on the bread side. (The pan should be medium, not too hot.) Then flip the fish over and cook for another 4 minutes, until it is just done. Meanwhile, combine the cabbage and the black-eyed peas together in a pot with as little juice as possible. Adjust the seasoning, if necessary.

Place a spoonful of garlic aioli onto each plate and smear with a spoon. Add olive oil as well. Fill a ring mold with the cabbage and black-eyed peas, pushing down lightly to be sure they hold their shape. Remove the ring and place a piece of mahi-mahi on top of the cabbage and black-eyed peas. Finish with a little salt and chives on top of the sourdough.

Ivory Salmon Tataki

SERVES 6

Tataki is a Japanese method of preparing fish. It involves quickly searing the fish on high heat on all sides, then marinating it. The result? Seared on the outside and raw on the inside, the salmon is light and delicious.

Ingredients

Salmon tataki
4 tablespoons Korean chili flakes

3 tablespoons white sesame seeds

2 tablespoons sesame oil

1 1/2 pounds ivory salmon, cut into
3/4-inch by 3/4-inch blocks

salt

Marinade
1/4 cup soy sauce

5 tablespoons white balsamic vinegar
or rice wine vinegar

2 tablespoons sambal

2 tablespoons sesame oil

Guacamole
3 avocados

1 small serrano pepper

1 tablespoon cilantro

1 lime, juiced

salt

Garnish
1/4 cup roasted hazelnuts

2 radishes, sliced

meat from 1/2 small young coconut

1/4 cup red shiso leaves

cilantro flowers

Instructions

For the salmon
Season the salmon with salt, Korean chili flakes, and sesame seeds. In a hot sauté pan (nonstick, if desired), add the sesame oil and the salmon. Cook on each side for approximately 20 seconds. Turn to the next side and repeat. (You want to sear the outside of the fish on all four sides.) The salmon should be in the pan only about 1 minute to 1 1/2 minutes. Then take it out and allow it to rest for 1 minute.

For the marinade
Meanwhile, place all the ingredients of the marinade into a shallow dish. (The salmon must fit.) Once the marinade is mixed well and seasoned, place the salmon inside the marinade. Leave the salmon in the marinade for 45 minutes. (If the marinade doesn't cover the salmon, that's okay. Simply turn it every 15 minutes.)

For the guacamole
Place all the ingredients into a food processor and purée until smooth. Season with salt and lime, and then put the purée into a small plastic pastry bag.

To finish
Cut the tip off the pastry bag and squeeze 5 dots of guacamole onto each plate. Then slice the salmon and place it on top of the guacamole. Add the roasted hazelnuts, radishes, and sliced young coconut meat next to each slice. Spoon some of the marinade around the fish. Finish with shiso leaves and cilantro blossoms.

Chili-Crusted Grouper with Mini-Blue Cornbread, Corn, and Avocado

SERVES 4

This dish pays homage to my Texas roots. Sometimes I crave Mexican food, and I first developed this recipe in an attempt to satisfy that urge. This dish has only a few components, so it comes together quickly. The versatile spice mix can be used on fish, chicken, and vegetables. Enjoy the contrast between sweet and spicy!

Ingredients

Mini-blue cornbread
1 cup plus 3 tablespoons milk
1 whole egg
1 stick butter, melted
1 1/8 cups all-purpose flour
1 1/8 cups blue cornmeal
3/4 cup sugar
1 teaspoon salt
1 tablespoon baking powder

2 extra large avocados, halved and grilled
3 tablespoons chili mix (2 ancho chilis, 2 pasilla chilis, 2 New Mexico chilis, 1/2 chipotle chili – all dried)

Grouper
4 tablespoons olive oil
1 pound grouper, cut into 4-ounce pieces
1/4 cup cilantro leaves
salt

Corn sauce
1 cup corn sauce (see page 54)

Instructions

For the mini-blue cornbread
In a large bowl, add the milk, egg, and melted butter. Stir well with a whisk, then add the rest of the dry ingredients and mix well. Spray a mini-madeleine pan with nonstick spray and spoon a little batter into each space (or alternatively, add to a hot cast iron skillet). Preheat your oven to 350 degrees, then place the batter into the oven for 15 minutes. Test with a cake tester until it comes out clean. Take out and set aside.

To finish
Cut the avocados in half and grill them for 3 minutes. Cut each half into four slices. Create your chili mix using dried, seedless peppers (2 ancho chilis, 2 pasilla chilis, 2 New Mexico chilis, 1/2 chipotle chili). Grind them in a spice grinder until they are coarse but not a powder. Drizzle half the olive oil onto the grouper, and then season the grouper slices aggressively with the chili powder mix and salt.

Place a large sauté pan with the remaining olive oil on medium heat. Add the grouper to the pan, cook it for 3 minutes, then flip it over to cook for another 4 minutes. Turn off the heat and allow the fish to stay hot. Place grilled, charred avocado slices onto each plate, and then place grouper next to the avocado. Add the corn sauce over the avocados. Finish with cilantro and mini-blue cornbread.

Mahi-Mahi with Eggplant, Apricot, Carrot, and Anasazi Beans

SERVES 4

The flavors of India subtly punctuate this dish. The beans and apricot sauce add an unexpected sensation. This recipe requires a little time to bring it together, but the complex flavors are sensational.

Ingredients

Eggplant
3 whole eggplants, peeled and sliced into rounds
5 tablespoons olive oil
1 lemon, juiced
salt

Anasazi beans
2 cups Anasazi beans
8 cups water
1/4 onion
salt

Apricot turmeric sauce
1 cup dried apricots
1/4 cup turmeric (3 large fingers), fresh, chopped, and peeled
1 teaspoon fresh ginger
1 tablespoon curry powder
4 cups water
salt

Instructions

How to roast eggplant

Peel and slice the eggplant lengthwise into 1/4-inch slices. Using a small round cookie cutter, cut small rounds of the eggplant, and then place them onto a sheet pan lined with parchment paper. Continue until you have cut all three eggplants. Set all the scraps of the eggplant aside for the curry sauce. Season the rounds well with salt, then drizzle them heavily with olive oil and lemon juice.

Place another piece of parchment paper on top of the eggplant. Place the sheet pan into an oven at 325 degrees for 20 to 25 minutes, or until the eggplant is soft but still retains its shape. (You do not want mush.) Take the eggplant out and allow it to cool. Once it is cool, you can flip it over with an offset spatula. This allows the top side to soak up any extra juice on the pan..

How to cook Anasazi beans

In a bowl of cold water, soak the Anasazi beans for 1 hour. Strain off the water. In a medium-sized pot, add the Anasazi beans with the fresh water and onion. Place on top of the stove on medium-high heat. Bring to a boil, then turn down to a light simmer and cover the pot. Cook for 30 minutes, then add 1 tablespoon of salt. Cook for another 30 minutes, or until the beans are tender and cooked through. Season a little more with salt, if need be. Set aside to cool.

How to make apricot turmeric sauce

Place all the ingredients except for the salt into a pot. Bring to a boil, then turn down to a simmer. Reduce by two thirds, and place into a Vitamix with a few pinches of salt. Purée until smooth. Taste and adjust the seasoning, if need be. (**Note:** this is a strong-tasting sauce on its own, but when it is paired with the rest of the ingredients, it complements well.) Place the sauce into a squeeze bottle once it has cooled.

continued.../

Mahi-Mahi with Eggplant, Apricot, Carrot, and Anasazi Beans

Eggplant curry sauce

1 1/2 cups eggplant (leftovers), chopped

1 teaspoon cumin

1 whole jalapeño pepper, sliced with seeds

1/2 can coconut milk

1 cup mint leaves

1 cup cilantro leaves

salt

Carrots

12 ounces globe carrots

1 1/2 cups water

1 teaspoon sugar

1 tablespoon butter

1 teaspoon salt

Mahi-mahi

3 tablespoons olive oil

1 tablespoon ras el hanout

4 pieces (5-ounces each) mahi mahi

1 ounce red vein sorrel

salt

How to make eggplant curry sauce

Cut the scraps of eggplant to form similar sizes and shapes. In a pot of boiling salted water (1 tablespoon of salt, 4 cups of water), cook the eggplant for 7 minutes. Strain out the eggplant and discard the water. Place the same pot back on the stove on medium heat and add the eggplant with the cumin and the jalapeño pepper. Cook for 1 minute, then add the coconut milk. Bring to a boil. Place everything into a Vitamix with the mint and cilantro. Purée until smooth and green (about 30 seconds). Season with salt and set aside..

How to cook carrots

Place the carrots into a small pot with all the other ingredients. Bring the pot to a simmer, and then cover it. Cook for 12 minutes. Using a cake tester, check to see whether the carrots are done. Cover and cook a few more minutes, if need be. Season and set aside.

How to cook mahi-mahi

In a large sauté pan, add 2 tablespoons of oil. Season the mahi-mahi with salt and ras el hanout on the fillet side. Place the fillet side down into the pan on medium-low heat, cover the pan, and cook the fish for 3 to 4 minutes only on the one side. When you see the fish is almost cooked on the fillet side, then flip it over and place the eggplant slices on top of the fish. Cook for 30 seconds, then take the fish and eggplant out of the pan.

Add a circular pattern of apricot sauce around each plate. Then place a spoonful of warm curry sauce in the middle. Place a few spoonfuls of the beans into the curry sauce. Place the mahi-mahi on top of the beans. Add a few carrots to the plate, and finish with red vein sorrel.

Presidents

I have never cooked for the president of the United States, but who knows, maybe I will in the future? Wouldn't that be a gig? Through the years I have cooked for governors, senators, and mayors. I have had the opportunity to prepare meals for presidents of companies, princes, musicians, and movie stars. And on one occasion, I cooked for the president of a Latin American nation.

Three-course lunch

Several years ago the Latin American president and his wife met with J.P. and Eloise for lunch. I prepared what I think of as a straightforward lunch menu with items in season, all favorites that taste great and have wide appeal. For the hors d'oeuvres I served duck potstickers. For the first course I made a porcini-mushroom-and-cheese tart with a light salad. Porcinis are fantastic mushrooms that are only in season for a short time during the year. The second course was a sous vide beef tenderloin with rutabaga and morels accompanied with beef au jus and chimichurri. I finished the luncheon with a parfait composed of a lemon biscuit, vanilla pastry cream, cherry compote, and Chantilly cream. I was happy that the lunch was well received and that my wife had the opportunity to meet the president.

Language not a barrier

During our interactions after lunch, the president and first lady were personable, genuine, thoughtful, and kind. Although I didn't have in-depth conversations with them, I left the occasion with those impressions. My Spanish should be flawless since my wife is from El Salvador, but I'm sad to say, it is not. However, the lunch that summer day was pleasant, my wife was there, and she was able to speak with the president and first lady – and to get a picture with them.

Sea Bass with Lentil, Curry, Cauliflower, and Cilantro

SERVES 4

This recipe takes a minimalist approach by including only a few ingredients, but really making each one shine. The jalapeño sauce gives the fish a jolt, while the curry adds depth to the lentils. This is a dish you'll want to prepare again and again!

Ingredients

Curry lentil purée

3 tablespoons olive oil

1 teaspoon ginger, fresh-minced

1 large orange bell pepper

1 1/2 tablespoons hot curry

1 teaspoon turmeric

1/2 cup red lentils

4 cups water

salt

Cauliflower

1/2 cauliflower head

2 tablespoons olive oil

1 1/2 teaspoons salt

pepper

Sea bass

3 tablespoons olive oil

1 pound sea bass, cut into 4-ounce pieces

5 tablespoons jalapeño cilantro pistou (see page 313)

dill

celery leaves

salt

Instructions

How to make curry lentil purée

In a small saucepot, add the oil, ginger, bell pepper, and a pinch of salt. Cook for 2 minutes, then add the curry and turmeric. Cook for 1 more minute, and then add the lentils, water, and another teaspoon of salt. Bring to a boil, then turn down the heat, cooking everything for 20 to 25 minutes, or until the lentils are thoroughly cooked. Drain off any excess water and reserve it for the purée. Place the lentils into a Vitamix, add a touch of the liquid, and purée until smooth. Season with salt, if needed. Set aside.

How to roast cauliflower

Preheat the oven to 350 degrees. Cut the cauliflower into big (1/2-inch) slices. You should have roughly 5 slices for a whole head of cauliflower. Then drizzle aggressively with olive oil, and add salt and pepper. Place in the oven for 15 to 17 minutes.

To finish

In a large sauté pan on medium heat, add the oil. Season the sea bass with salt. Place the sea bass fillet-side down (the side seasoned with the salt). Season the bottom side of the fillet with salt as well. Cook for 6 to 7 minutes on the one side. The fish should be cooked almost all the way through on that side. Then flip the bass over, add a spoonful of jalapeño cilantro pistou, and cook for 1 more minute. Turn off the heat. Add a spoonful of curry lentil purée onto each plate. Add a few pieces of cauliflower next to the purée. Place the sea bass next to the purée with another drizzle of pistou. Finish with dill and celery leaves, if desired.

Black Bass with Roasted Figs, Urad Gota, and Beurre Rouge Sauce

SERVES 4

I love the delicate flavor and texture of black bass. It has the versatility to take on many different flavor profiles. For this recipe, I pair it with carrots, leeks, chimichurri, and urad gota. (The urad gota is also known as the matpe bean or black lentil, although it isn't a true lentil, but a husked bean.) It is the perfect accompaniment for the fish. The bean has great flavor and texture, I like its size, and it cooks really fast. I finish this dish with a fig-and-balsamic red wine butter sauce for a little sweetness.

Ingredients

Urad gota

1 cup whole urad gota, without the husks

1 leek top

2 cloves of garlic

1 fennel top

2 teaspoons salt

3 tablespoons butter

2 tablespoons olive oil

2 carrots, peeled and finely diced

1 leek, small-diced

2 tablespoons chimichurri

pepper

Beurre rouge sauce

1 cup red wine

1 cup balsamic vinegar

1 teaspoon sugar

1/3 cup cream

1 stick butter

salt

Blue potato chips

5 fingerling purple potatoes, sliced thin and fried

1 1/2 cups vegetable oil

salt

Instructions

How to make urad gota

Soak the urad gota in a bowl with 3 cups of water for 20 minutes (or more, if you have time). Strain off the water, and then place the urad gota into a medium-sized pot. Add 3 cups of water, 1 leek top, 2 garlic cloves, 1 fennel top (optional), and salt. Bring to a boil, cover, and turn down to a simmer. Cook for 15 to 20 minutes, or until the urad gota becomes tender (think rice or beans).

Strain off the water and discard the leek, garlic, and fennel. Lay the urad gota flat on a sheet pan lined with parchment paper to cool down. Then place the pot back onto the stove. Add the butter, olive oil, diced carrots, leeks, and a pinch of salt. Cover and cook for 5 minutes. Add the cooled down urad gota. Cook for 2 minutes, and add the chimichurri. Season with salt and pepper, set aside, and keep warm.

How to make beurre rouge sauce

Place the red wine, balsamic vinegar, sugar, and cream into a small pot on medium heat. Reduce by two thirds, or until the sauce is thick (almost like syrup). Add the butter. Season with salt, and keep warm.

How to make blue potato chips

Slice the potatoes thin. In a small pot, add vegetable oil for frying and bring to 315 degrees. Add the potatoes in small batches, making sure not to add too many, which would overcrowd the pan. Fry until crisp. Strain out and season immediately with salt.

continued.../

Black Bass with Roasted Figs, Urad Gota, and Beurre Rouge Sauce

Black bass

10 black mission figs

3 tablespoons olive oil

2 whole black bass, filleted

chervil sprigs

salt and pepper

How to cook black bass

Place the figs into a heat-proof pan, add one 3-ounce ladle of the beurre rouge sauce over the top, and roast in an oven at 400 degrees for 10 minutes. In a cast iron or nonstick pan on medium-high heat, add the olive oil. Season the fish with salt on the skin side. Season with salt and pepper on the fillet side. Place the bass skin-side down in the pan. Push down slightly with a spatula or another smaller pan on top of the fish for 15 seconds until the fillet doesn't curl up, but lies flat in the pan. Cook for 5 minutes.

Meanwhile, using a ring mold, add a few scoops of the urad gota to each plate, pushing down tightly to shape the beans. Add the fried blue potato chips on top. Flip the fish over for 20 seconds, and then take it out, placing the bass on the plate next to the urad gota. Take the roasted glazed figs out of the oven and place them next to the fish. Finish with a ladle of the beurre rouge sauce around the plate. Garnish with chervil.

Seared Kampachi with Kiwi, Sweet Potato, and Hatcho Miso

SERVES 4

Hawaiian Kampachi is prized for its buttery flavor and crisp, clean bite. It is one of my absolutely favorite fishes to prepare. Here I combine it with pickled golden kiwi, roasted sweet potatoes, and an aged hatcho miso. This recipe skates through a lot of Pacific rim countries to pull together ingredients that come together in perfect harmony. Get on board and take a ride to flavor town!

Ingredients

Hawaiian Kampachi
12 ounces Hawaiian Kampachi loins
1/3 cup Korean red chili flakes
3 tablespoons sesame seeds
3 tablespoons olive oil
salt

Kiwi pickle
2 kiwis, quartered and sliced
1 cucumber, quartered and sliced
2 radishes, sliced
1/2 cup seasoned rice wine vinegar
2 teaspoons salt

Hatcho miso
1/4 cup hatcho miso
1/2 cup mayonnaise or Vegenaise

Sweet potatoes
3 tablespoons olive oil
2 Japanese purple sweet potatoes, roasted
salt

Instructions

How to cook Kampachi
Season the Kampachi with salt, Korean chili flakes, and sesame seeds. In a hot sauté pan (nonstick if desired) add the oil and the Kampachi. Cook on one side for approximately 5 to 10 seconds. Repeat until you have seared all four sides. The Kampachi should be in the pan only 20 to 30 seconds total. Then take it out and allow it to rest. Once it has cooled, you can slice the Kampachi into 1/4-inch pieces.

How to make kiwi pickle
Place all the ingredients into a bowl and allow them to marinate for at least 30 minutes.

How to make hatcho miso
Place all the ingredients into a bowl and whisk until everything is well incorporated. Then pour the mixture into a squeeze bottle and set it aside until you are ready to use it.

How to roast sweet potatoes
Preheat your oven or grill to 375 degrees. Drizzle olive oil onto the sweet potatoes, and season them with salt. Place the sweet potatoes into your Big Green Egg or oven for about 45 minutes, or until they are soft and tender all the way through. Take them out and allow them to cool.

continued.../

Seared Kampachi with Kiwi, Sweet Potato, and Hatcho Miso

Peppadew® gel

12 Peppadew® peppers

1 1/4 cups water

1 teaspoon agar-agar

salt

Garnish

4 tablespoons olive oil

1/2 cauliflower, cut into small pieces

1 tablespoon furikake seasoning

1 golden kiwi, sliced thin

chervil

salt

How to make Peppadew® gel

Place Peppadew® peppers and water into a Vitamix and purée until smooth. Strain into a small saucepot. Add the agar-agar to the pot and bring it to a boil, stirring continually. Cook for 5 minutes. Season with salt, and then pour the gel into a half sheet pan or baking dish. Place it into the refrigerator until the agar-agar has set. Then take a knife and cut the set gel into sections. Place it all into a Vitamix and purée until smooth. Pour it into a squeeze bottle and set it aside until you are ready to use it.

To finish

In a bowl add olive oil, cauliflower, and your favorite furikake seasoning, along with a pinch of salt. Toss well and place onto a sheet pan lined with parchment paper. Roast for 13 to 15 minutes in an oven preheated to 400 degrees. Take it out and allow it to cool. Then add your hatcho miso and Peppadew® to each plate in a decorative manner. Add the roasted cauliflower, Kampachi slices, and sliced golden kiwi. Add a slice of the warm purple sweet potato, and add the pickled kiwi next to it. Finish with chervil!

Wild Sea Bass with Porcini and Truffle

SERVES 4

This recipe embraces the change from spring to summer. Truffles and porcinis are the prized mushrooms of Italy and can be used in so many different ways. I use both in this dish. It might seem like overkill, but the result is delicious!

Ingredients

Truffle sauce
1 black truffle
11/2 cups really good chicken stock
2 tablespoons butter
salt

Porcini mushrooms
8 ounces porcini, quartered
2 tablespoons olive oil
2 tablespoons butter
pepper

Beans
1 cup yellow wax beans, blanched
1 cup haricots verts, blanched
1 teaspoon garlic, minced
2 tablespoons olive oil
salt and pepper

2 tablespoons olive oil
4 pieces sea bass (5 ounces each)
1 ounce watercress sprigs
salt

Instructions

For the truffle sauce
Place the truffles, hot chicken stock, and a pinch of salt into the Vitamix. Purée for 2 to 3 minutes, then add the butter. Adjust the seasoning, and set aside.

For the porcini mushrooms
Quarter the porcini lengthwise and place them into a sauté pan on medium heat with 2 tablespoons of oil and 2 tablespoons of butter. Sauté for 5 minutes, and then flip them over to cook another 5 minutes, allowing the mushrooms to brown and to become tender. Season with salt and pepper, and keep warm.

For the beans
Blanch the beans in boiling, salted water (1 tablespoon of salt, 4 cups of water) for 3 minutes. Then strain out and place the beans into a sauté pan with the garlic and olive oil. Cook for 2 minutes, season with salt and pepper, and keep warm.

To finish
In a sauté pan on medium-high heat add the oil. Season the bass with salt on both sides and place the pieces fillet-side down in the pan. Cook for 5 minutes on that side. Flip the pieces over and allow them to cook for 1 minute. Remove the fish from the pan. Place the beans on each plate, adding a few slices of porcini on top. Place the bass onto the plates and ladle a generous amount of truffle sauce over them. Finish by adding watercress sprigs.

Hamachi Tartare
with Chinese Celery

SERVES 4

I love this recipe simply because it makes me happy. This is a great way to start any dinner party and impress your guests! The starter is both light and refreshing, and it owes its flavor to the green broth and hamachi.

Ingredients

Hamachi

1 tablespoon cherry-shaved wood chips

1 tablespoon oak-shaved wood chips

1 pound hamachi (sushi-grade yellowtail)

4 tablespoons Chinese celery, minced

1 tablespoon furikake rice seasoning (nori, bonito, and sesame)

1 teaspoon sansho pepper

1 to 2 tablespoons tamari

1 teaspoon sesame oil

1/2 teaspoon salt

Green juice

1 cucumber, juiced

1 bunch of celery, juiced

1 tablespoon rice wine vinegar

1 teaspoon salt

2 sprigs of lemon verbena

Garnishes

3 radishes, sliced thin

broccoli flowers

micro cilantro

Meyer lemon oil

Instructions

For the hamachi

Fill a medium-large plastic ziplock bag with ice. Set up your stove-top smoker by placing the wood chips into the bottom of the pan. Turn the heat on until the wood shavings start to smoke, and then place the rack and tray on top of the wood chips. Put the ice bag down on the tray and place the hamachi on top of the ice bag.

Place the cover on top, or use foil. Let the fish smoke for 1 minute on high heat, and then turn off the heat and allow the fish to absorb the smoke inside the smoker for the next 30 minutes with no heat. The ice helps ensure that the fish won't cook. (What you're doing is adding a very subtle smoke flavor to the fish.) After the fish has absorbed the smoke, take it out and place it back into the refrigerator for 30 minutes.

Remove the hamachi, small dice it, and place it into a bowl. Add the minced Chinese celery, furikake, sansho, tamari, sesame oil, and salt to the fish. Mix well with a spoon and adjust the seasoning, if needed. Set aside in the refrigerator.

For the green juice

Run the cucumber and celery through a vegetable juicer. Season with rice wine vinegar and salt. Add the lemon verbena to the juice to add a little subtle flavor. Set aside in the refrigerator for at least 30 minutes.

To finish

For each serving bowl place a round cookie cutter (or ring mold) in the middle. Fill the ring mold with a few spoonfuls of the hamachi tartare, pressing down with the back of the spoon so it is tight and holds its shape. Place the sliced radish on top. Remove the ring mold and pour some of the green juice into the bottom of the bowl. Garnish with broccoli flowers and micro cilantro. Finish with a drizzle of Meyer lemon oil.

Everything Bagel Crepe with Smoked Salmon and Sauce Gribiche

SERVES 6–8

Here's a fun twist on a classic. This great appetizer or brunch recipe is easy to make and captures all of the flavors of bagels and lox without the carbs! It's addictive and absolutely delicious!

Ingredients

Crepe batter
1 1/2 cups milk
2 eggs
1 1/4 cups flour
1 teaspoon salt
1 tablespoon poppy seeds
1 tablespoon sesame seeds
1 tablespoon garlic, dried and minced
1 tablespoon onion, minced
1 teaspoon black pepper
1 tablespoon butter

Sauce gribiche
4 egg yolks, hard-boiled
1 egg yolk, raw
1/2 tablespoon Dijon mustard
3 tablespoons pickle juice
1/2 cup olive oil (or vegetable oil)
2 tablespoons parsley, finely chopped
2 tablespoons dill, finely chopped
2 tablespoons chives, finely chopped
splash of water, if needed
salt and pepper

4 ounces spreadable cream cheese
1 lemon, zested
1/4 cup capers
1 pound smoked salmon
2 ounces caviar
(salmon would be a great alternative)
1/8 cup dill

Instructions

For the crepe

In a bowl add the milk and eggs. Whisk well. Then add the flour, salt, and spices. Mix well. The batter should be slightly thick and without lumps, but not nearly as thick as a pancake batter. In a small sauté pan (9 inches), add a little butter. Put on medium-high heat.

Spoon 1 ladle (2 to 3 ounces) of batter into the center of the pan, and then twirl the pan in a clockwise motion to distribute the batter evenly throughout. Let the batter cook for 30 seconds until it is golden brown, then flip it over. Cook for another 5 to 10 seconds, and then place the crepe onto a sheet pan lined with parchment paper. Continue the process until all the crepes are cooked.

How to make *sauce gribiche*

Place the hard-boiled yolks, raw yolk, mustard, and pickle juice into a blender. Purée until smooth. While running the blender, add the oil in a smooth, slow, steady stream until the sauce emulsifies. Season with salt and pepper, and fold in the chopped herbs. Add more pickle juice or salt, if need be. Set aside for later.

To finish

Spread a thin layer of cream cheese on half of a crepe. Add a little lemon zest and caper to the cream cheese, then add 2 to 3 ounces of smoked salmon on top of the cream cheese. Roll the crepe up into a tight roll. Cut the ends off at an angle (bias) and cut each crepe in half at an angle, making the appetizer-sized pieces all about the same length. Continue the process with the remaining crepes. When you're ready to serve, add some *sauce gribiche* on top of each slice of crepe, and also to the plate. Top with caviar and dill.

Get the Led Out

What if you learned that the lead singer for one of the world's best known rock bands was coming for lunch? To top that, what if your wife's due date for your first child had come and gone? That was the scenario one day late in winter.

I used to listen to a lot of classic rock when I was in my late teens and early 20s, during my tenure as a cook in the restaurant business, so I was excited to cook for a Led Zeppelin band member. On the other hand, I was also wondering whether I'd get a call letting me know that my wife was in labor. That was an emotional juggernaut.

Lunch

I started the lunch with a duck confit salad with beets, avocado, and a Barolo truffle vinaigrette. This was a great way to ease into the meal. Next, because I had Meyer lemons that I wanted to use, I made sunchoke-ricotta gnocchi with Meyer lemon sauce that was light, bright, and delicious! I added hedgehog mushrooms for an added depth of flavor.

Not long before this lunch I had eaten an amazing dessert at the Latymer, a Michelin-starred restaurant in London, so I decided to recreate it. The restaurant served a pistachio financier with raspberry and other accoutrements. (Financier is a browned butter almond cake popular in France.) I substituted pistachios for almonds and made the traditional browned butter cake, adding raspberries, candied pistachios, and pistachio ice cream.

The food was wonderful and lunch was exciting for all of us. The timing was wonderful as well because I never did get the call about my wife that day. We actually had to wait another week for my son to be born. It was such a joy to be there for that life-changing moment.

Seared Flounder with White Bean, Fava, and Duck Bacon

SERVES 4

The inspiration for this dish comes from the traditional French cassoulet. The bacon and bean marriage is one that is tried and true. For this dish I kept the wild flounder simple and seasoned it only with salt and pepper. The fava beans and duck prosciutto added depth.

Ingredients

White beans

1 pound white beans (soaked in water at least 1 hour, if you have the time)

1/2 charred onion

3 cloves of garlic

1 sprig of rosemary

8 cups water

2 teaspoons salt

Flounder

3 tablespoons olive oil

4 fillets flounder

salt and pepper

Fava beans

2 tablespoons olive oil

1/4 cup duck bacon or prosciutto, diced

1/2 onion, diced

2 cloves of garlic, minced

1 cup fava beans, blanched

1 tablespoon sherry vinegar

salt and pepper

Garnish

olive oil

cilantro flowers or rosemary

Instructions

How to cook white beans

Soak the white beans in water (at least 1 hour, if you have the time). Drain them and place them with all of the other ingredients into a soup pot. Place the pot on top of the stove on medium-high heat. Bring to a boil, and then turn down to a light simmer and cover. Cook for 30 minutes or so, then add the salt.

Continue to cook for another 25 to 30 minutes, or until the beans are just tender all the way through. At this point I like to pour the beans into a shallow baking dish to cool, but I don't strain out the cooking liquid. You want to stop the cooking process so they don't overcook and become mush. Set aside to cool.

To finish

In a large sauté pan on medium-high heat, add 2 tablespoons olive oil along with the duck bacon. Cook for 3 minutes, then add the onion and garlic to the pan along with a pinch of salt. Cook for another 2 minutes, and then add 2 cups of cooked white beans to the pan along with a little of the bean water.

Bring to a boil, and allow the beans to cook for 2 minutes. Add the fava beans with a few splashes of the sherry vinegar. Season everything with salt and pepper. Cook for 1 more minute, and adjust the seasoning, if need be.

continued.../

Seared Flounder with White Bean, Fava, and Duck Bacon

In another large sauté pan on medium heat add 3 tablespoons of olive oil. Season the flounder with salt and pepper, and then place each fillet face down into the pan. Cook for 4 minutes on the fillet side. Flip the flounder over and cook for another 30 seconds on the bottom side.

Place each flounder fillet onto a plate to keep it from overcooking. Spoon the bean ragout into each individual serving bowl with some of the juice. Place the fish on top. Drizzle everything with olive oil and herb flowers, if desired.

Corvina with Radishes, Beans, and Romesco Sauce

SERVES 4

I enjoy making everyday food special. Corvina is a firm, white fish with a mild, sweet taste. I begin this dish by cooking Oaxacan and black coco beans, and combining them with tarragon, vinegar, and a little duck fat. Next I char red poblano peppers on the grill and purée them into a romesco sauce. I finish the corvina with a garlic confit butter and blanched radishes.

Ingredients

Oaxacan beans

1 1/2 cups fresh Oaxacan beans

5 cups vegetable stock

1 onion, charred

1 sprig of thyme

1 bay leaf

2 cloves of garlic

2 teaspoons salt

Black coco beans

1 1/2 cups black coco beans, fresh

1/2 onion, charred

2 cloves of garlic

4 cups water

1 bay leaf

1 teaspoon salt

Red poblano romesco sauce

4 red poblano peppers, grilled (plus 1/2 red serrano pepper, optional)

1/4 cup Marcona almonds

1 clove of garlic

1 tablespoon Parmesan cheese

1 cup olive oil

salt

Instructions

How to cook Oaxacan beans and black coco beans

Place the Oaxacan beans with all of their associated ingredients into one pot, and the black coco beans and their ingredients into a separate pot. Put both pots on top of the stove on medium-high heat. Bring them to a boil, and then turn down to a light simmer and cover. Cook for 20 to 25 minutes, or until the beans are tender and cooked through. (If the beans are dry rather than fresh, you will need twice as much time to cook them.) Set aside to cool.

How to make red poblano romesco sauce

Char the red poblano peppers on the grill, and then peel and deseed them. Place all the ingredients into a blender except for the olive oil and salt. Pulse a few times to get everything blended, and then turn on high and drizzle the olive oil in until you get a smooth purée. Finish with salt and set aside for later.

Radishes

2 baby purple radishes,
sliced thin and blanched

2 baby green daikon radishes,
sliced thin and blanched

2 baby watermelon radishes,
sliced thin and blanched

Garlic confit butter

1 cup garlic, peeled

2 cups vegetable oil

4 tablespoons butter

1/2 teaspoon salt

Corvina

2 tablespoons olive oil

1 1/2 pounds wild corvina,
cut into 4 equal portions

1 cup black coco beans, cooked

1 cup Oaxacan beans, cooked

1/2 cup cooking water

1 to 2 tablespoons sherry vinegar

1 tablespoon tarragon, chopped

3 tablespoons duck fat

salt

Garnish

chive oil (see page 316)

cilantro

How to cook the radishes

Place of pot of salted water (1 tablespoon of salt, 4 cups of water) onto the stove and bring it to a boil. Add the sliced purple radishes, cooking them about 30 seconds. Strain out the radishes and place them into an ice bath. Continue the same process with the green daikon radishes and the baby watermelon radishes.

How to make garlic confit butter

Place the garlic cloves and vegetable oil into a small pot. Bring to a hard simmer, and then turn down to low. (The oil should just barely bubble.) Cook for 30 to 45 minutes, or until the garlic is a light golden brown. Cool completely. Once the garlic is completely cooled, strain most of the oil out, then add the butter and salt. Purée the butter and garlic together to get a smooth garlic butter. Set aside until ready to use.

How to cook corvina

In a medium-hot sauté pan, add the olive oil. Season the corvina pieces with salt and place them fillet-side down in the pan. Cook on that one side for 4 minutes. Meanwhile, place all the cooked beans into a small pot with 1/2 cup of the cooking water. Bring to a boil, then add the vinegar, tarragon, and duck fat to the beans. Cook until the beans are completely warmed through and most of the liquid is evaporated. Season with salt and pepper, if need be.

To finish

Add a large spoonful of the romesco sauce to the bottom of each individual serving bowl. Place a few spoonfuls of beans on top of the sauce.

Flip the fish over and spread a thin layer of the garlic butter on top of the seared fillet. Add the slices of radish on top of the butter. Season the radishes with a pinch of salt. Let the fish cook for another minute or so, and then take it out of the pan.

Place the corvina on top of the beans. Drizzle chive oil around each bowl. Add a few pieces of cilantro around the bowl.

Miso Black Cod

SERVES 4

Most high-end Japanese restaurants have some version of miso-glazed black cod on their menus. I decided to make my version of it with hoisin sauce, an Asian barbecue sauce. The glaze includes three ingredients – hoisin, miso, and pickled ginger juice. If you can't find pickled ginger juice, simply add lime, or water, to thin the sauce slightly. I serve this cod over a bed of rice and cabbage. Uncomplicated and mouthwatering!

Ingredients

Chicken ssamjang broth
3 ounces ginger, sliced
1 whole onion, sliced
2 whole carrots, sliced
3 tablespoons sesame oil
1 whole serrano pepper, sliced
8 cloves of garlic, sliced
1 chicken carcass (bones), roasted
10 cups water
1 cup soy sauce
1/4 cup ssamjang (spicy fermented soy bean paste)

Braised cabbage
2 tablespoons butter
2 tablespoons olive oil
1 teaspoon ginger, minced
12 ounces shiitake mushrooms, sliced
1 small cabbage, julienned
salt

Jasmine rice
3 cups water
2 slices ginger
1 teaspoon salt
1 1/2 cups jasmine rice

Instructions

For the chicken ssamjang broth
Put the ginger, onion, and carrots into a pot with the sesame oil and cook for 10 minutes. Next, add the serrano pepper and the garlic. Cook for another 3 minutes, then add the rest of the ingredients. Bring the pot to a boil.

Turn down the heat and allow everything to simmer for a few hours. Once you have a deep, rich, flavorful broth – and it has reduced down by more than half – the broth should be ready. Adjust the seasoning with salt and / or spice to your liking.

For the cabbage
Add the butter, oil, ginger, sliced mushrooms, and half of the julienned cabbage to a braising pan heated to medium. Add a pinch of salt to the cabbage, then add the rest of the julienned cabbage on top and add another pinch of salt. (Adding salt and covering the pot sweats the vegetables. Salt draws water out of the vegetables so they cook in their own liquid.) Keep an eye on maintaining medium heat so the vegetables don't burn. After a 25-minute sweat, the cabbage should be tender and melt in your mouth.
Set aside and keep warm.

For the rice
Place 3 cups of water into a pot with the ginger and salt. Bring to a boil, then pour the rice in and give it a few stirs with a spoon. Allow the water to come back to a boil, cover the pot, and turn down to low. Cook for 18 to 20 minutes, then turn off the heat. Try not to lift the lid to check the rice as it is cooking because you allow the steam to escape from the pot. Once the rice is done, allow it to steam for another 5 minutes and then use.

continued.../

Miso Black Cod

Hoisin-miso glaze

2 tablespoons miso

5 tablespoons hoisin sauce

1 tablespoon pickled ginger juice or lime juice

Black cod

1 1/2 pounds black cod, cut into 5-ounce pieces (skin and bones removed)

3 tablespoons olive oil

salt

Garnish

1 pinch togarashi chili

1 ounce Thai basil leaves

8 garlic chive flowers

For the hoisin-miso glaze

Place all the ingredients into a bowl and whisk well. Set aside until you're ready to use.

To finish

Season the black cod with salt on both sides. In a medium hot sauté pan add the oil and black cod. Cook for 4 minutes, until the sides of the fish start to brown and crispen. Flip the cod over and spoon the hoisin-miso glaze over each piece of cod. Turn the heat down slightly and allow the fish to cook for another 2 to 3 minutes. Turn the pan off and let the fish rest while you plate up the dish.

Place a round ring mold in the bottom of each serving bowl. Scoop out the rice and fill half of the mold with rice. Next, fill the other half of the ring mold with your cabbage-and-mushroom mix. Using the back of your spoon, push down on both the rice and the cabbage to make them tight. Remove the mold. Take the black cod out of the pan, then place it on top of the rice and cabbage. Add the chicken ssamjang broth around the bowl. Finish the fish with a sprinkle of togarashi, Thai basil, and garlic chive flowers.

Redfish with Fermented Daikon Radishes and Everything Sauce

SERVES 4

The redfish is nothing short of amazing! The amount of moisture it retains makes it very easy to cook, and therefore it's very easy to fall in love with this fish. The skin is a little thicker than most fish, but cooked properly, it becomes a great natural crust. The fermented daikon radishes and fish sauce take this to the next level. (Note: Wild-caught redfish cannot be sold commercially, so you'll have to buy farmed fish.)

Ingredients

Fish sauce

1 fish carcass

1 chicken bone, roasted

4 beef bones, smoked

1/2 cup miso

3 tablespoons soy sauce

1/2 fennel bulb (or 1 cup fennel, chopped)

1 onion

1 leek

2 carrots

3 stalks celery

1 large ginger finger, sliced

2 jalapeño peppers, halved

6 cloves of garlic

2 bay leaves

10 cups water

1 tablespoon peppercorns

To finish the fish sauce

2 tablespoons cornstarch

3 tablespoons water

splash of black vinegar

splash of soy sauce

salt

Instructions

How to make fish sauce

Rinse the whole fish carcass well under cold water to get rid of any blood. (Blood will turn your stock cloudy.) Place the carcass into a pot with the rest of the fish sauce ingredients, except what you will use to finish the sauce, and bring to a boil. Turn down to a simmer, and reduce by at least half. The stock should have a deep, rich flavor. (If the stock still tastes very mild and watery, then reduce a little more until you have a deep, rich flavor profile.)

Strain out and discard the contents, then take the fish stock and place it back into a pot to thicken with a cornstarch-and-water slurry. Simmer for 10 minutes, and add a splash of vinegar, soy sauce, and salt. Set aside and keep warm.

How to ferment daikon radishes

In a bowl, place the daikon radish shavings and mix them well with salt. Next, put them into a glass jar, covering them with a piece of parchment paper or a coffee filter the same size as the mouth of the jar. Place a small weight on top of the paper or filter inside the jar to push the radish shavings down. (The weight will keep the shavings submerged in their own liquid as they start to release it.) Close the lid.

An alternative and easy way of doing this if you don't have a commercial weight is to fill your jar 3/4 full with radishes. Place a small piece of parchment paper on top. Next, place a freezer bag or sturdy food grade bag into the jar. Fold the top of the bag around the outside of the jar, then fill the bag with water almost to the top of the jar. The water will act as your weight. Close the lid.

continued.../

Redfish with Fermented Daikon Radishes and Everything Sauce

Fermented daikon radishes

1 pound daikon radishes, peeled and shaved

2 teaspoons salt

Redfish

3 tablespoons olive oil

20 ounces redfish (4 pieces)

salt and pepper

Mushrooms

2 tablespoons butter

2 tablespoons olive oil

8 ounces maitake mushrooms

salt

Garnish

Thai basil leaves

Keep the jar away from direct sunlight. (If you close the lid tightly, remember to release the lid every day or every other day to release the pressure that builds up.) The longer you ferment the radishes, the more intense the flavor becomes. You can set the jar aside anywhere from 2 days to 2 weeks. I opt for 3 to 5 days.

To finish

In a cast iron or nonstick pan on medium heat, add olive oil. Season the redfish with salt on the skin side. Season with salt and pepper on the fillet side. Place the fish skin-side down in the pan. Push down with the back of your metal spatula or fish weight for 15 to 20 seconds, or until the fillet won't curl up any more and lies flat in the pan. Cook for 5 minutes on the skin side.

Meanwhile, in another small pan on medium-high heat, place the butter, olive oil, and mushrooms. Season lightly with salt and cook for 5 minutes. Flip the fish over and cook for 20 seconds. Add the mushrooms to the middle of each individual serving bowl (four portions). Pour a ladle of the fish sauce next to the mushrooms. Then place the redfish on top of the sauce. Add the fermented radish shavings on top of the mushrooms. Garnish with a few Thai basil leaves.

Snapper with Habanero Leche de Tigre

SERVES 6

Leche de tigre, literally "tiger's milk," is the citrus-based, spicy marinade used to cure the fish in classic Peruvian ceviche. I serve this dish as a crudo, but you could easily use the marinade to "cook" the fish. This is an exciting and refreshing starter that you will really enjoy!

Ingredients

Leche de tigre

2 cups vegetable stock

1 habanero pepper, without seeds

1 whole serrano pepper, with seeds

2 cups celery, including green leaves and stems

1/2 cup cilantro

3 cloves of garlic

1 stalk lemongrass

3 large lemons, juiced

6 ounces snapper scraps

salt

Snapper crudo

1 avocado, diced

1 baby fennel, shaved

1 Fuji apple, small-diced

1 pound Pacific snapper, sliced thin

3 tablespoons green garlic oil (see page 316)

2 radishes, sliced

chive blossoms

3 tablespoons cilantro stems, chopped

salt

Instructions

How to make leche de tigre

Place all of the ingredients into a blender and purée until smooth. Strain through a fine mesh sieve, and then place into the refrigerator.

How to make snapper crudo

Place the avocado, shaved fennel, and apple all around each bowl. Then place your fish on top. Season with salt and pour the leche de tigre all around the bowl. Finish with green garlic oil, radishes, chive blossoms, and cilantro stems.

Kampachi Poke with Nasturtiums

SERVES 4

I was inspired to create this recipe when I noticed the nasturtiums in full bloom. Nasturtiums have a distinct peppery flavor and grow like weeds, spreading their vines without boundaries. I use them raw, simply stuffed with Kampachi tartare (or poke). The combination of the raw, fatty Kampachi with the peppery flowers is not only appealing to the eyes, but also to the taste.

Ingredients

Kampachi tartare (or poke)
8 ounces Kampachi, small-diced
3 tablespoons green onion, chopped
1 tablespoon cilantro, chopped
2 tablespoons sesame seeds
1/4 teaspoon sansho pepper
1/2 teaspoon salt
1 tablespoon sesame oil
1 teaspoon sriracha sauce
1 tablespoon soy sauce
1/2 avocado, small-diced
2 tablespoons nori komi furikake
24 nasturtium flowers and petals

Instructions

How to make Kampachi tartare (or poke)
In a small mixing bowl add all the ingredients, mix well, and season. Allow the mixture to marinate for at least 30 minutes.

To finish
Stuff each nasturtium flower with 1 to 2 teaspoons of the Kampachi poke. Place 1 petal and 2 stuffed flowers (or as many flowers as you want) on each serving plate.

Coriander Sea Bass
with Chanterelles and Carrots

SERVES 4

I prepared this simple sea bass dish using just a few ingredients. The crust on the fish is one of my favorite go-to spices – crushed coriander seeds. The coriander has almost a floral or a perfume aroma to it, and the flavor is amazing! Coriander is the seed of the cilantro plant, which, in my opinion, has a much different flavor. The sauce takes a bit of time, but you could easily substitute a simple pan sauce. Coriander can enhance almost any protein or vegetable, converting it into a fantastic delight!

Ingredients

Reduction sauce

1 cup fish carcass, bones, and skin

bones of 1 whole chicken, roasted

4 whole beef bones, smoked or roasted

1/2 cup miso

3 tablespoons soy sauce

1/2 cup fennel, chopped

1 whole onion, chopped

1 whole leek, chopped

2 whole carrots, chopped

3 stalks celery, chopped

6 cloves of garlic

2 bay leaves

1 tablespoon peppercorns

10 to 12 cups water

2 tablespoons cornstarch (with 3 tablespoons water)

1 splash sherry vinegar

3 tablespoons soy sauce

salt

Carrots

1 pound carrots, roasted and sliced

salt and pepper

Instructions

How to make the reduction sauce

Have your butcher fillet the sea bass, if you don't know how. Ask for any fish bones or scraps the shop would normally throw away. Rinse those scraps, bones, and skin well under cold water to get rid of any blood. (Blood will turn your stock cloudy.)

Place the fish bones and scraps into a pot with the rest of the reduction sauce ingredients (except the cornstarch, vinegar, soy sauce, and salt) and fill it with water. Bring the pot to a boil. Turn down to a simmer, and reduce by at least half. The stock should have a deep, rich flavor. (If the stock still tastes very mild and watery, then reduce it a little more, perhaps to two thirds, until you have a deep, rich flavor profile.)

Strain out, discarding the contents, and then pour the fish stock back into a pot to thicken with a cornstarch-and-water slurry. Simmer for 10 minutes, then add a splash of vinegar, soy sauce, and salt. Set aside and keep warm.

For the carrots

Season the carrots with salt and pepper, or any other spice you have on hand. Once you have roasted and cooled the carrots, you can cut them into 1/4-inch thick slices.

continued.../

Coriander Sea Bass with Chanterelles and Carrots

Sea bass

4 tablespoons olive oil

1 pound sea bass, cut into 4 pieces

2 tablespoons coriander seed, crushed

1 pound chanterelle mushrooms, washed and dried

3 tablespoons butter

salt

Garnish

3 tablespoons carrot microgreens

How to cook sea bass

In a large sauté pan on medium heat add 2 tablespoons of oil. Season the fillet side of the sea bass with salt and coarse coriander. Place the sea bass fillet-side down to season the bottom side with salt.

Cook for 4 to 5 minutes on one side. The fish should be cooked almost all the way through, depending on how thick the piece is. (If you have a really thick piece, flip the sea bass over and place it into an oven preheated to 400 degrees. Leave it for 5 minutes, and then take it out. It should be done.) Turn the fish over to cook for 1 more minute. Turn off the heat.

Meanwhile, in a small sauté pan add the chanterelles with 2 tablespoons each of butter and oil. Cook for 7 minutes, then add the roasted, sliced carrots. Cook for another 3 to 4 minutes, and then add 1 tablespoon of butter.

To finish

With a spoon, distribute the vegetables among 4 bowls. Spoon the sauce over the vegetables. Remove the fish from the pan and lay it on top of the vegetables. Finish with the carrot microgreens.

Black Bass with Trumpet Mushrooms and Artichokes

SERVES 4

Light and absolutely delicious! The combination of artichokes and mushrooms with turnip purée is an earthy way to balance out this dish.

Ingredients

Mushrooms
10 ounces Trumpet Royale™ mushrooms (also called king trumpet mushrooms)
3 tablespoons olive oil
3 tablespoons butter
salt and pepper

Turnip purée
4 turnips, peeled and diced
1 potato, peeled and diced
4 tablespoons butter
1/8 cup cream
salt and pepper

Parsley oil
2 small bundles flat-leaf parsley
1 cup vegetable oil
1 teaspoon salt

Instructions

For the Trumpet Royale™ mushrooms
Cut your mushrooms in half lengthwise, and then place them into a sauté pan with 3 tablespoons of oil and 3 tablespoons of butter. Sauté them for 10 minutes on medium heat. Allow the mushrooms to brown and to become tender. Season with salt and pepper, and keep warm.

For the turnip purée
Place the turnips and the potato into a pot and fill it with water. Add salt, bring to a simmer, and cook for 20 to 25 minutes, or until both the turnips and the potato are cooked through. Strain off the water, and then put the turnips and potato into a Vitamix or food processor. Add the butter and cream, and then purée until smooth. Add a little butter, salt, or pepper, if desired. Set aside and keep warm.

For the parsley oil
In a pot of boiling salted water (1 tablespoon of salt, 4 cups of water), blanch the parsley tops for 20 seconds. Place them into an ice bath immediately. Drain off and squeeze out the excess water. Add 1 cup of vegetable oil and 1 teaspoon of salt. Purée for 30 to 45 seconds, or until the blend is bright green. Run the contents through a chinois or fine-mesh strainer. Let the contents drip through the strainer – don't push the pulp through so you will have a clear oil with no pulp. Place the oil into a squeeze bottle and set aside.

continued.../

Black Bass with Trumpet Mushrooms and Artichokes

Red pepper romesco sauce

3 garlic cloves

1 jar red bell peppers, roasted (or 3 large peppers, roasted)

1 Fresno chili pepper (jalapeño or serrano for heat)

1/3 cup roasted marcona almonds (or any other nut)

1 1/2 cups olive oil

1/4 cup Parmesan cheese (or Manchego)

salt

Black bass

3 tablespoons olive oil

1 whole black bass, filleted (4 fillets of 5 ounces each)

salt and pepper

Artichokes

5 baby artichokes, cooked and quartered (see page 61)

Garnish

4 green olives, sliced

12 sprigs of chervil or parsley

For the red pepper romesco sauce

Put the garlic, roasted red peppers, Fresno chili pepper, and almonds into the blender. Pulse a few times to get everything blended, and then turn on high, drizzling the olive oil in until you have a smooth purée. Finish with the cheese and salt. Purée until smooth. Add seasoning, if needed, and set the sauce aside until you are ready to use it.

To finish

In a cast iron or nonstick pan on medium heat, add the olive oil. Season the black bass with salt on the skin side. Season with salt and pepper on the fillet side. Place the skin side down in the pan. Push down slightly for 15 seconds, or until the fillet won't curl up any more and lies flat in the pan. Cook for 5 minutes.

Meanwhile, dip some red pepper romesco sauce onto each plate, placing a few pieces of the mushrooms and artichokes around. Add a spoonful of the turnip purée. Flip the fish over and let it cook 20 seconds, and then put each black bass serving onto a plate next to the purée. Finish with olive slices, parsley oil, and chervil (or parsley leaves).

a: with Eloise at Fox 7 in Austin

b: with JP at Mobile Loaves & Fishes in Austin

c: with my sous chef sons

d: with JP before we take flight

e: with Sara Slaughter at Faraday's Kitchen Store

f: concentrating on plating

g: with Peter Finkbeiner (food critic)

Traditionally, main courses are built around the meat dish. The meat takes center stage on the plate like a star in a Broadway production. When the star gives a good performance, the show is well received. But if the star's performance is mediocre, the show has little chance to succeed. The same principle applies to meat preparation.

With the recipes in this section, I offer you a wide range of techniques and flavor profiles to add to your repertoire. Keep in mind the following concepts. First, aggressively season meat. Thick cuts of meat require even more seasoning because the seasoning doesn't penetrate to the center. Remember this when serving sliced meat – you may need to sprinkle more salt on each individual slice.

Second, avoid overcooking meat. It is always better to undercook slightly, allowing a margin of error so you can correct the error than allowing yourself no margin at all. It is also absolutely crucial to rest the meat, especially steaks, to retain tenderness and juiciness. It is best to cook your meat to 90 percent of the desired internal temperature. Next, allow it to rest for 5 to 10 minutes. Remember that when you stop the cooking process, the meat will continue to cook for at least another 5 degrees.

Third, add more flavor by introducing meat to fire, wood, or smoke, or a combination of the three. I use the Big Green Egg when grilling or smoking. If all you have is a gas grill, add some wood chips, or cold smoke the meat first, then grill it. Following these basic concepts will turn any meat into the star of your meal!

MEAT

Seared Foie Gras with Fig and Orange

SERVES 4

This tasty appetizer is what I like to call "gourmet in minutes!" These classic French flavors work together well. You will need sourdough bread, fig jam, foie gras, and an orange.

Ingredients

8 ounces foie gras

2 tablespoons butter

5 tablespoons olive oil

4 slices sourdough bread or raisin bread

4 ounces fig jam

orange zest from 1 whole orange

3 tablespoons chives

salt and pepper

Instructions

Cut 4 portions of foie gras, trying to remove as much of the blood vein as possible from the liver. (You can score the foie gras with the back of a knife if you want to elevate your presentation.) Season with salt and pepper.

Meanwhile, in a large sauté pan, add the butter and the olive oil. Place 4 slices of bread into the pan, and toast them on medium heat for 2 to 3 minutes, or until the first side is golden brown. Flip the bread over, and season with salt while the second side toasts (2 minutes). Remove the bread from the pan. Take that same pan off the heat, and then add the foie gras to the pan. The pan should be hot, but not smoking hot.

Place the pan back onto the heat, cooking one side of the foie gras until it turns a dark brown and a natural crust forms. Flip the foie gras and cook it 1 more minute. The foie gras should cook in about 2 to 3 minutes. When touching the foie gras with your finger, like checking whether a steak is done, the foie gras should feel soft on the outside, but a little firm in the middle.

When you take the foie gras out of the pan, place it onto a plate. (A restaurant would have it on a paper towel to soak up any extra fat. Since this recipe calls for the fat to drain into the bread, there is no need to drain it.) Add a layer of fig jam to each slice of bread, and then add the seared foie gras. Finish with orange zest, chives, and a few grains of flaked salt. Serve immediately.

Whole Roasted Jamaican Jerk Chicken

SERVES 6

For this jerk chicken recipe, instead of using a dry rub, I use a wet marinade that takes only 5 minutes to make. The marinade can also be used on a variety of different proteins, and you'll fall in love with it. I would highly recommend cooking this chicken in a Big Green Egg or other smoker. The result will transport you instantly to Jamaica!

Ingredients

Jamaican jerk marinade (enough for 2 whole chickens)

1/2 cup soy sauce

8 cloves of garlic

1 tablespoon fresh ginger

1/2 onion

1 teaspoon dried oregano

1 tablespoon allspice

1 teaspoon cloves

1 tablespoon paprika

1 teaspoon nutmeg

1/2 cup orange juice

1/2 cup vegetable oil

1 tablespoon cinnamon

4 habanero peppers

2 serrano peppers

1 tablespoon sugar

1/4 cup sherry vinegar

Chicken

2 whole chickens

Instructions

For the marinade

Place all of the ingredients into a blender and purée until smooth.

How to cook the chicken

Place the chicken into a large plastic bag and pour the marinade over it. Allow at least 2 hours to marinate, if you have the time. Then on a sheet pan or roasting pan lined with foil or parchment paper, pour the contents of the bag and add 1 cup of water. Season the chicken with salt all over and place the pan into an oven preheated to 400 degrees.

Cook for roughly 1 1/2 hours, or until the internal temperature of the chicken thigh reaches 165 degrees. Take the chicken out and allow it to rest for 20 to 30 minutes. (If the top of the chicken looks like it is starting to burn while roasting, simply place a piece of foil over the top to prevent any more darkening.) Once the chicken has rested, serve and enjoy!

Lamb Shank with Pistachio, Dill, and Moussaka

SERVES 4

Sometimes I'm just in the mood to prepare a certain cuisine, and that was the case when I first created this dish. I love Mediterranean flavors, specifically Greek. This recipe calls for braising a lamb shank with a light sauce of dill and pistachios. It also includes one of my favorite ragouts, known as moussaka, which mainly consists of eggplant, tomatoes, and herbs.

Ingredients

Lamb
4 large lamb shanks
salt and pepper

Braising liquid
2 tablespoons olive oil
1 onion, chopped
2 leek tops
1 garlic bulb
2 sprigs of dill, chopped
2 fresh bay leaves
2 tablespoons dried Greek oregano
2 carrots, chopped
2 celery stalks, chopped
1/2 cup pistachios
1 fennel top, chopped
1 lemon, zested and juiced
stock or water to fill (2 quarts)

Pistachio sauce
3 cups braising liquid
1/4 cup parsley leaves
1/4 cup of dill sprigs
1/2 cup roasted pistachios
lemon (optional)
salt

Instructions

How to braise lamb shanks
Season the lamb with salt and pepper, and place it into a medium-hot braising pan with the olive oil. Sear on the first side for 4 minutes, then flip the lamb shanks, adding all the other ingredients except the water. Cook for 4 to 5 minutes so all the aromatics can start to release their flavors. Then add the water and bring the pan to a boil. When it boils, turn down to a very light simmer (barely bubbling) and cover. Cook for roughly 2 1/2 hours, or until the meat is completely tender. Then let the shank stay in the liquid. (If you take it out of the liquid, it will dry up.)

How to make pistachio sauce
Take 3 cups of the braising liquid, along with some of the cooked leeks, onions, garlic, and cooked pistachios from the braising liquid. Add to them the parsley and the extra dill and pistachios. Purée everything in a Vitamix for 1 1/2 minutes, or until the mixture is bright green and smooth. Season the sauce with salt and lemon, if need be. Set aside and keep warm.

continued.../

Lamb Shank with Pistachio, Dill, and Moussaka

Beluga lentils

2 cups water or vegetable stock

1/2 cup beluga lentils

1 sprig of thyme

2 cloves of garlic

1 teaspoon salt

splash of sherry vinegar
(added at the finish)

1 tablespoon butter
(added at the finish)

1 tablespoon olive oil
(added at the finish)

Pita bread

1 package yeast

1 teaspoon sugar

1 cup warm water

3 1/2 cups all purpose flour

2 teaspoons salt

1/4 cup yogurt

2 tablespoons honey

6 ounces butter, melted

1/4 cup olive oil
(for cooking the pita in the pan)

How to cook beluga lentils

Place all the ingredients except the sherry vinegar, butter, and olive oil into a pot and bring it to a boil. Turn down to a simmer and cover with a lid. Cook the lentils for 25 to 30 minutes, until they are tender all the way through but not overcooked. Strain out the liquid and reserve it. Then pour the lentils onto a sheet pan lined with parchment paper (if you are preparing them ahead of time) and allow them to cool completely.

How to make fresh pita bread

For the dough, add yeast and sugar to warm water to activate the yeast. Mix well with a fork and then let the mixture sit for at least 5 minutes. In another bowl, add flour and salt. Make a well in the center of the flour and pour in the activated yeast mixture. Add the yogurt, honey, and butter to the center well, and using a fork, mix the wet ingredients with the dry ingredients. When the dough begins to come together, finish mixing with your hands to bring the dough completely together. (Or use your mixer with a dough hook to make the dough.)

After the dough has come together, knead it for 5 minutes, and then let it rise in a covered bowl for 1 hour. Punch down the dough, and if you have time, let the dough rise again. If you don't have time for a second rise, portion the dough into 3-ounce pieces and let them rest for 20 minutes, covered. With a little dusting of flour, roll out the portions into round pita shapes about 1/8-inch to 1/4-inch thick.

In a large sauté pan on medium-high heat, add 1/2 teaspoon of olive oil for each piece of bread. Once the pan is hot, put 1 rolled out pita bread into the pan. Cook for 30 seconds, or until golden brown, and then flip it, sprinkling it on top with a little salt. Cook for another 45 seconds, and then take it out to cool, or keep it warm in a towel or bread warmer. Continue the process, adding oil as needed, until you have cooked all the pita.

Lamb Shank with Pistachio, Dill, and Moussaka

Moussaka

1/4 cup olive oil
1 onion
1 fennel, sliced
2 eggplants, peeled and cut into large bâtonnets
1 teaspoon chili flakes
5 cloves of garlic
5 heirloom tomatoes (or 1 box of Pomi tomatoes)
2 tablespoons chopped dill
1 tablespoon Greek oregano
salt and pepper

Yogurt

(optional side)

Garnish

3 tablespoons pistachios
3 sprigs of dill

How to make moussaka

In a large saucepot on medium-high heat, add the olive oil, onion, fennel, and eggplant. Cook for 4 to 5 minutes, and add the chili flakes and garlic. Cook for 2 minutes, then add the tomatoes and a good healthy pinch of salt (1 teaspoon) along with the herbs.

Bring to a boil and then turn down to a simmer. Cover and cook for 30 minutes, stirring occasionally. After 30 minutes, check to see whether the eggplant and all the other vegetables have become very tender. Check the seasoning. Season until you have good flavor. Keep warm.

To finish

Take the shanks out of their braising liquid. Strain off the stock and reserve for another recipe (maybe a lamb pasta). Place the shanks back into the braising pan you just strained out and place the pistachio sauce on top of the shanks. Turn the heat on and cook for just 1 minute to make sure the lamb shank is completely hot.

Place your lentils into a sauté pan with a little of the cooking water and bring to a boil. Season with a touch of sherry vinegar, salt, pepper, and maybe a touch of olive oil or butter. Ladle a large spoonful onto each plate, and then add moussaka next to the lentils. Take your shanks out of the pistachio sauce and place them on top of the vegetables. Add a little extra sauce on top. Garnish the top of the shank with pistachios and dill. Serve with pita (and a side of yogurt, if desired).

Rib Eye with Hato Mugi and Sunflower

SERVES 4

Hato mugi is a grain that is often referred to as Job's tears. Since ancient times it has been prized for its medicinal properties, and it has a sweet, nutty taste. This grain is a millet, but it can be used like a barley. I think it pairs well with grilled ribeye steak, garlic, and onion.

Ingredients

2 rib eye steaks, each 1-inch thick

Rib eye marinade
1 tablespoon sesame oil
1/4 cup soy sauce
1 orange, juiced

Green garlic butter sauce
1 cup green garlic bottoms, chopped
1 cup white wine
1/2 cup cream
1 cup green garlic tops, blanched
1 stick butter
salt

Hato mugi
2 tablespoons olive oil
1/2 onion, small-diced
1/2 cup celery, small-diced
1 cup hato mugi, rinsed
1 teaspoon orange zest
1 tablespoon barley miso
(more if needed)
2 tablespoons blond miso
1/4 cup sunflower seeds
4 cups chicken stock
salt

Instructions

How to marinate steaks

Place all the ingredients into a ziplock bag and let the steak marinate for at least 2 hours.

How to make green garlic butter sauce

In a small saucepot, add the green garlic bottoms and white wine. Cook until there is just a small amount of white wine left in the bottom of the pot. Then add cream to the pot and bring it to a simmer. Cook until you have half the cream left, then pour everything into a Vitamix along with the blanched garlic tops. Purée everything until it is smooth, and then add your butter cube by cube into the Vitamix until all the butter has been incorporated. Season with salt and strain, if desired. Set aside and keep warm.

How to cook hato mugi

In a small saucepot, add the olive oil, onion, and celery. Cook for 5 minutes, then add the hato mugi, together with the zest, both misos, sunflower seeds, and chicken stock. Bring to a boil, cover, and turn down to a simmer. Cook for another 20 to 25 minutes, or until the hato mugi is tender and cooked all the way through. Once it is cooked, season it lightly with salt, if needed. Keep warm.

continued.../

Rib Eye with Hato Mugi and Sunflower

Garlic confit

2 cups garlic cloves, peeled

2 cups vegetable oil

Garlic miso purée

1 cup garlic confit

1/4 cup miso

1/4 cup water

1/4 cup leftover garlic oil

Garnish

sunflower sprouts

For the garlic confit

Place both the garlic cloves and the oil into a small pot. Bring to a simmer, and then turn down low. Cook the garlic for 25 to 30 minutes, or until the garlic has turned a light golden brown (not dark). Take the pot off the heat and allow it to cool completely.

For the garlic miso purée

Strain out 1 cup of the garlic confit and add it, together with the miso paste, into a Vitamix. Add some water, and then purée. If the purée is too thick, you can add some more water, and you can add a touch of garlic oil as well.

Season with salt, if needed. You should have a good balance of both garlic and miso. One flavor should not dominate the other, but you should have a good mixture of both. Set the purée aside.

How to grill ribeye

Set the temperature of your grill to 350 degrees, or thereabouts, with wood in your grill. Take the steaks out of the marinade and season them with salt and pepper. Place them onto the grill and cook for 1 1/2 minutes, then flip the steaks. Cook for another 1 1/2 minutes, and then flip the rib eyes again. Repeat this process 3 to 4 more times, or until your steaks are medium rare inside. (This technique of continual flipping, called a reverse sear, is foreign to the old-school way, but as you can see in the picture on page 210, the rib eye almost looks like it was prepared sous vide. Continual flipping prevents either side from cooking too long so you can avoid having browned, overcooked edges on your steaks. To see a video tutorial, go to www.saltvanilla.com.) Take the rib eyes off the heat and brush them with 2 spoonfuls of garlic miso purée. Allow them to rest for at least 5 to 10 minutes.

To finish

Place a spoonful of green garlic butter sauce down onto each plate. Add a spoonful of the hato mugi. Then slice the steaks and place them on top of the hato mugi. Add some more garlic miso purée onto the middle of each slice, and then top with with sunflower sprouts.

Beef Two Ways for Royalty

SERVES 4

I created this dish as the last savory course for a royal dinner (see the story on page 216) – and it was a good one. I chose the tenderloin and rib cuts, then marinated each in with different ingredients. Chimichurri was my choice for the tenderloin and a Korean barbecue marinade for the short ribs. I paired the smoked ribs with a corn purée and black garlic ketchup. I smothered the tenderloin in a truffle sauce. Truly decadent!

Ingredients

3 pounds short ribs, on the bone

Short rib marinade
1 cup orange juice

1/2 cup soy sauce

3 tablespoons gochujang

1 finger ginger, sliced

2 cloves of garlic

1 cup water

salt

Tenderloin
1 pound fillet of beef tenderloin,
cut into 3 steaks
(roughly 5.5 ounces each)

2 tablespoons chimichurri for
marinade (see page 316)

salt and pepper

Truffle sauce
2 cups really good chicken stock
(see page 317)

1 cup beef stock

1 large black truffle (2 ounces)

4 tablespoons heavy cream (optional)

3 tablespoons butter

1 splash sherry vinegar

salt and pepper

Instructions

For the short ribs
Place all the ingredients except the salt and the water into a blender. Purée until smooth. Place the ribs into a heatproof pan and pour the marinade over them. Let the ribs sit in the marinade for about an hour. Season the beef ribs with salt, then pour a cup of water into the bottom of the pan. Bring your Big Green Egg or smoker up to 285 degrees. Place the ribs into the smoker and smoke them for roughly 6 to 7 hours, basting them periodically, until the internal temperature reaches 185 to 190 degrees.

For the tenderloin
Place the steaks into a ziplock bag with 2 tablespoons of chimichurri. Allow the steaks to marinate for at least 1 hour and as much as 4 hours. Take the steaks out of the marinade and season them with salt and pepper. Place them onto the grill and cook for 1 1/2 minutes, then flip the steaks. Cook for another 1 1/2 minutes, and flip the steaks again. Repeat the process 5 or 6 more times, and then take them off the heat and allow them to rest. (This technique of continual flipping is called a reverse sear, as explained on page 212.)

For the truffle sauce
Place both the chicken stock and the beef stock into a pot with the truffle and a pinch of salt. Bring to a boil, then turn down to a simmer. Reduce the liquid by half. Pour the stocks and black truffle into a blender and purée until smooth (20 seconds). While the blender is running, add the cream (optional) and butter. Adjust the seasoning with salt, pepper, and a splash of sherry vinegar. Set aside and keep warm.

continued.../

Beef Two Ways for Royalty

Corn purée

1 1/2 cups white corn juice
(6 corn cobs)
1 teaspoon lime juice
salt

Black garlic ketchup

(see page 314)

For the corn purée

Place the corn juice and a pinch of salt into a saucepot. Place the pot on medium heat and whisk often to prevent scorching. The corn juice will thicken up from the natural starch and sugars, and it will become thick. (This process takes about 8 minutes, depending on your level of heat.) Season with salt and lime, if desired. Set aside and keep warm.

To finish

Place both meats back onto the grill or into an oven for a few minutes, just to heat them up if they aren't warm anymore. Place a spoonful of the corn purée onto each plate. Baste the short ribs, and then put a small piece on top of each spoonful of corn purée. Slice the tenderloin, placing a slice next to the short rib on each plate. Spoon the truffle sauce over the top of the tenderloin. Add a spoonful of the black garlic ketchup to the plate. Grate a little fresh truffle, if you have it, on top of the tenderloin.

Royal Dinner

JP told me that a royal couple would be coming to dinner and that it would be just the four of them. I have always tried to be professional, and I have not been one who is star struck, but this dinner was kind of a big deal.

It was the day before the dinner and I needed to decide quickly what I would prepare for them. I was told they eat almost anything except sea urchin. No problem there. I know I wanted to make at least a few vegetarian courses. I also thought that they must have eaten a thousand formal dinners in their lives, and I certainly didn't want to make this dinner stuffy. I wanted the dinner to be elegant, but not formal. Most important, the dinner needed to be delicious!

Fish Taco?

With a quick search, I discovered that a fish taco is one of the favorite foods for one of them. Could that possibly be an option for one of the courses?

In my younger years I would have tried my hardest to impress the guests with as many different techniques and ingredients as possible. But now I recognize that events like this are a chance to let my creativity and skills shine. In the end, it always comes down to pleasing the guests.

Taking Chances

In this case I took a bit of a chance by serving a fish taco for the fourth course. I made onion ash tortillas and filled them with chili-crusted sea bass, rémoulade, guacamole, salsa, poblano aioli, and cabbage slaw. It was a calculated risk that paid off. The couple raved about the tacos.

Unforgettable

With any meal I always wonder how things will turn out for the guests. Every meal I try to put forth my best effort. I was really surprised when the prince made a point of coming into the kitchen to thank me personally. He popped in as I was cleaning up and said, "I just want to thank you for a fantastic meal – it was really great!" That was a night to remember!

Dinner Menu

FIRST

"avocado toast" – tuna, avocado, fried rice, kimchi aioli, and ponzu

(I used a triangular mold to layer these ingredients in flavor to appear as an avocado toast.)

SECOND

summer beans, morels, onions, and chicken truffle broth

(see page 63)

THIRD

roasted beet salad with Marcona almonds, manouri cheese, radishes, and nasturtium dressing

(a light salad that everyone really enjoyed)

FOURTH

chili-crusted sea bass taco with guacamole and slaw

(homemade ash tortilla, chili-seared sea bass, caper rémoulade, and jicama cabbage slaw)

FIFTH

Beef Two Ways with corn and black garlic

(see page 213)

SIXTH (choice of dessert)

chocolate, banana, and peanut butter bomb

classic vanilla crème brûlée

pear and almond financier with pear sorbet

Beef Stir-Fried Rice Bowl

SERVES 4

Every chef needs at least a couple of recipes that turn leftovers into something interesting. This tasty recipe for beef stir-fried rice is one of mine. Comfort food defines this dish in a nutshell!

Ingredients

Stir-fried rice

4 cups white basmati rice, cooked

6 tablespoons sesame oil

4 eggs

2 teaspoons ginger, minced

1 small onion, small-diced

2 carrots, small-diced

2 teaspoons garlic, minced

1 pound leftover steak, diced
(filet mignon, brisket, flank etc. –
if using fresh meat, use the marinade
for the short ribs on page 213 for
at least 45 minutes)

1 tablespoon spicy kimchi paste

1/3 cup soy sauce

1 cup frozen peas

2/3 cup green onion, chopped

1 tablespoon sriracha sauce

12 ounces fresh mung bean sprouts

4 tablespoons chopped cilantro

salt

Garnish

2 tablespoons Korean chili flakes

4 tablespoons sesame seeds, toasted

1 cup micro cilantro

Instructions

How to make stir-fried rice

Start by making rice, following the instructions on the package of whatever rice you decide to use. I prefer basmati because of the flavor and the lack of starch it has compared to other rices. Once the rice is cooked, pour it out onto a sheet pan to cool immediately. (Having cold, leftover rice is ideal because it has already dried out.)

Wok cooking is all about high heat and speed. Most home stoves don't have the heat capabilities, but you can still achieve a great fried rice.

In your wok (or large pan) on the highest heat, add 2 tablespoons of sesame oil. Beat your eggs in a bowl. When the oil is just about to start smoking, add the eggs to the wok. They should immediately start to bubble up around the edges. Using a wok spatula or spoon, scramble the eggs. (This should take only about 15 seconds.) When they are cooked, slide them off onto a plate and chop them roughly.

Place the wok back onto the fire and add the remaining sesame oil, along with ginger, onion (not the green onion), carrot, and a pinch of salt. Cook for 1 minute, then add the garlic and the beef. Cook for 1 more minute, and add the rice. Cook the rice for 5 minutes, then add the kimchi paste and soy sauce. Cook for 2 to 3 minutes.

Add the peas, 1/3 cup of green onions, and the cooked eggs, then cook for another minute. Add another pinch of salt, if need be, along with a little bit of sriracha sauce. Taste the rice to see what it needs. If nothing, add the bean sprouts and chopped cilantro to the rice and turn off the heat. Stir one or two more times to incorporate everything. Distribute the rice among 4 different bowls. Top with Korean chili flakes, sesame seeds, the remaining 1/3 cup of green onions, and the micro cilantro.

Beef Tenderloin with Olive and Potato

SERVES 4

Steak, potato, onions, and olives – what more do you need? These are flavors that I love together. The two olive sauces in this recipe are quick and easy to prepare. They can be made ahead of time and served at room temperature. This is a modern take on meat and potatoes.

Ingredients

Green olive sauce
1 cup water
1 cup Castelvetrano olives, pitted
2 ounces chives, blanched
1 clove of garlic
4 tablespoons olive oil
1/2 teaspoon xanthan gum

Kalamata olive sauce
1 cup water
1 cup Kalamata olives, pitted
2 tablespoons olive oil
1/2 teaspoon xanthan gum

Potatoes and onions
1 1/2 pounds peewee potatoes
12 ounces pearl onions
4 tablespoons olive oil
2 sprigs of rosemary
salt and pepper

Instructions

How to make the green olive sauce
Place the water, olives, chives, and garlic into a Vitamix. Purée until smooth. Add the olive oil in a slow, steady stream, then add the xanthan gum in the same slow and steady stream. Purée for another 15 seconds. The sauce should be thickened slightly. Place it into a container and set it aside.

How to make the Kalamata olive sauce
Place the water and olives into a Vitamix. Purée until smooth. Add the olive oil in a slow, steady stream, then add the xanthan gum in the same slow and steady stream. Purée for another 15 seconds. The sauce should be thickened slightly. Place it into a container and set it aside.

For the potatoes and onions
Place the potatoes and onions onto a sheet pan or roasting pan. Drizzle them with 4 tablespoons of olive oil, and season them with salt, pepper, and chopped rosemary. Roast the potatoes and onions in your Big Green Egg (or oven) at 400 degrees for about 30 minutes, or until they are tender and cooked through. Remove, and allow them to cool. Peel the outer layer of the pearl onions and season them with salt again. Set aside.

Steaks

1 pound beef tenderloin, cut into
4-ounce steaks before cooking

salt and pepper

Castelfranco greens

How to grill fillet

Set your grill or Big Green Egg to 300 degrees. Season the steaks with salt and pepper. Place them onto the grill (or into your Big Green Egg) and cook for 1 1/2 to 2 minutes. Flip the steaks. Cook for another 1 1/2 to 2 minutes, and then flip the steaks. Repeat the process 3 to 4 more times. Flip and repeat until your fillet is medium rare inside. (This technique of continual flipping is called a reverse sear, as explained on page 212.)

Remove the steaks from the heat and allow them to rest for at least 5 to 10 minutes. Slice the steaks, and then place them onto each plate, along with potatoes and onions. Add the olive sauces, and finish with Castelfranco greens.

Quail with Fennel and Turnip

SERVES 8

I'm always on the lookout for alternatives to red meat. Here is a very French-style quail dish that is both tender and full of flavor. When I first prepared this recipe, it was one of six courses, and the only meat, that I served. If you are looking for an advanced recipe, this one is for you!

Ingredients

14 whole quail, legs cut off, thigh meat for mousse, and breast deboned with skin intact

Quail thigh mousse
6 ounces thigh meat
1 clove of garlic
1 teaspoon fresh tarragon leaves
1 egg white
1/4 cup cream
salt and pepper

Quail breasts
14 double quail breasts (28 total), deboned with skin intact
3 tablespoons butter

Quail jus
16 quail carcasses
1 leek
2 carrots
2 celery stalks
1 small fennel
1 onion
2 tablespoons olive oil
6 cloves of garlic
2 bay leaves
1 sprig of thyme
1 sprig of oregano
2 cups red wine
12 to 14 cups water
2 tablespoons cornstarch for slurry
2 additional tablespoons water for slurry
salt

Instructions

For the quail thigh mousse
Make sure all the equipment and food is very cold. (Place them into the freezer for 15 minutes.) Take some of the leg meat off the bone and place it into a food processor along with the garlic and tarragon. Purée until smooth. Then, while the food processor is still running, add the egg white and drizzle in the cream. Season with salt and pepper, and then place into the refrigerator.

For the quail breast
Place the deboned quail breasts skin-side down onto your cutting board. There should be 2 breasts from each quail. Spoon or pipe the thigh mousse into the middle of the 2 quail breasts. Using plastic wrap and your hands, roll the quail up into a tiny log with the skin on the outside and the breast and filling on the inside. Roll as tight as possible, tie or twist both ends, and then place into a sous vide bag. Repeat until you have all of the breasts (14 total) filled and rolled. Seal the sous vide bag airtight with 3 tablespoons of butter. Place the sous vide bags into the refrigerator for 1 hour to firm up, if you have the time. Next, place them into a 135-degree water bath for 45 to 55 minutes. Remove them from the water bath, and allow them to rest.

For the quail jus
Place the bones onto a sheet pan and brown in an oven at 400 degrees for 30 to 45 minutes. In a stockpot with 2 tablespoons of olive oil, brown the vegetables until they are caramelized. This should take about 15 minutes. Add the garlic and herbs, and cook for another few minutes, then add the bones to the pot, along with the wine, and reduce by half.

continued.../

Quail with Fennel and Turnip

Fennel purée

1 tablespoon olive oil

2 tablespoons butter

2 large fennel bulbs, sliced thin

1 to 2 tablespoons cream

salt

Roasted fennel

1 large fennel, sliced thin

3 tablespoons olive oil

1 sprig of savory

salt and pepper

Turnips

1 cup baby turnips

28 quail legs (from which the thigh meat was removed)

1 clove of garlic

1 sprig of thyme

1 bay leaf

1/2 teaspoon salt

1 cup duck fat

Garnish

fennel pollen

Meanwhile, deglaze the sheet pan with some water to get all of the bits of quail off it, and then pour that water into the pot. Fill the pot with the rest of the water. Bring to a boil, then turn down to a simmer. Reduce by 3/4. Thicken the jus slightly with a cornstarch slurry by slowly pouring it into the stock and stirring continuously with a whisk. Cook for another 5 to 10 minutes. Season with salt, strain, and set aside. Keep warm.

For the fennel purée

In a large sauté pan on medium heat add the olive oil, butter, sliced fennel, and 1/2 teaspoon of salt. Cover and cook for about 25 minutes, stirring occasionally to ensure even cooking. The fennel should not have any color when it is done. Try not to brown the fennel as you are cooking it so your purée will be cream-colored. You can add the 1 to 2 tablespoons of cream at the end of the cooking process. Once the fennel is done, place it into a Vitamix and purée it until smooth. Adjust the seasoning, if need be, set aside, and keep warm.

For the fennel

Place the fennel onto a sheet pan and drizzle with olive oil. Season with salt, pepper, and a sprig of savory. Place into the oven. Roast for 15 minutes, then flip the fennel over. The fennel should be golden brown. Roast on the other side for another 10 to 15 minutes, or until the fennel is tender.

For the turnips

Place the baby turnips and the quail legs into a small pot, along with the garlic, herbs, 1/2 teaspoon of salt, and the duck fat. You are essentially preparing the legs in the style of confit with turnips added to the pot. Bring to a boil, and then turn down to a very, very soft simmer. Cover the pot and allow it to cook for 20 to 25 minutes, or until the turnips and legs are tender all the way through. Set aside, and keep warm.

Quail with Fennel and Turnip

To finish

In a sauté pan on medium heat, add 2 tablespoons of the duck fat from the cooked legs and turnips. Take the quail breasts out of the bag and remove the plastic wrap. Season the breasts with salt and pepper. Place them into the pan along with the confit legs to brown on all sides. This should take about 3 to 5 minutes. Take the breasts and legs out of the pan and let them rest on a cutting board. Meanwhile, place a spoonful of fennel purée onto each plate with some of the roasted fennel and turnips. Cut the very ends off each quail breast log to stabilize them on the plate. If the logs are tiny, just place them onto the plates. If they are big or long, then cut them in half before placing them onto the plates. (This is why the recipe calls for 14 breasts – some might be really small, but others might need to be cut in half, so there would be some left over.) Place 3 pieces of breast on each plate, along with 2 legs. Finish with some of the jus, and garnish with fennel pollen.

Thai Green Curry Quail with Noodles

SERVES 4

This is a great Thai green curry recipe I once served to Wolfgang Puck, but without the noodles (see pages 247). I have been making this satisfying dish for years. At first glance, the long list of ingredients might seem intimidating, but don't be scared away. The recipe calls for galangal root, which is sometimes hard to find. (Ginger is a great substitute because the two are closely related.) Usually you would serve curry with rice, but when I created this dish, I had rice noodles on hand, so I used them instead.

Ingredients

Thai green curry sauce

2 tablespoons sesame oil

1/2 onion, sliced

5 cloves of garlic, chopped

1 finger ginger, sliced

1 finger galangal root
(if you can find it), sliced

1 lemongrass stalk, chopped

3 Kaffir lime leaves

1 cinnamon stick

1 teaspoon whole allspice

2 pieces star anise

1/4 cup palm sugar (or regular sugar)

1/4 cup green curry paste

2 cans coconut milk

1/2 cup cilantro leaves

1/2 cup mint leaves

1/2 cup Thai basil leaves

2 teaspoons fish sauce

Instructions

For the Thai green curry sauce

In a medium saucepan on medium heat, add the sesame oil, onion, garlic, ginger, galangal root, lemongrass, Kaffir lime, cinnamon, allspice, and star anise. Cook for 5 minutes on medium to low heat. You do not want to brown the vegetables, but you do want them to release all their flavor. Once you have sweated the vegetables, add your sugar and green curry paste. Cook for 2 minutes, then add the coconut milk. Bring to a boil, and then turn off the heat. Allow to cool for 4 minutes. Strain out the sauce and add it to a blender, discarding all of the vegetables and spices. Add 1/2 cup each of cilantro leaves, mint leaves, and Thai basil leaves. Blend until the mixture is smooth and bright green (35 seconds). Finish with 2 tablespoons of fish sauce. Set aside to cool to room temperature.

continued.../

Thai Green Curry Quail with Noodles

Quail

8 quail, deboned

2 tablespoons soy sauce

2 cloves of garlic, chopped

1 lime, juiced

1/4 cup Thai green curry sauce

1 package vermicelli rice noodles

8 ounces shiitake mushrooms, sliced

1/2 onion, sliced

5 baby carrots, blanched
and oblique-cut

1 cup of cilantro leaves, Thai basil,
and mint, mixed

2 tablespoons sesame oil

To marinate the quail

Place the quail into a ziplock bag with the soy sauce, 1/4 cup of the cooled Thai green curry sauce, the garlic, and the lime. Let the quail marinate for 1 to 2 hours in the refrigerator.

Meanwhile, in a pot of boiling, salted water (2 tablespoons of salt, 12 cups of water), cook the rice vermicelli noodles for 3 to 4 minutes, or until tender and cooked through. Strain off and place into an ice bath to stop the cooking.

To finish

Preheat the grill. Take the quail from the refrigerator 30 minutes early so it can return to room temperature. In a large sauté pan on high heat, add the sliced shiitake mushrooms. Cook for 3 minutes, or until they start to brown, and then add the onion. Cook for 2 more minutes, then add the carrots and noodles. Add 1 cup of the Thai green curry sauce and cook for 3 minutes, or until all is incorporated and hot.

Lightly season the quail with salt, and grill the quail for 2 to 3 minutes on high heat on each side. Take the quail off the grill and let it rest for 5 minutes. Finish the noodles with a cup of mixed herbs and a pinch of salt, if needed. Place a portion of noodles down into each individual bowl. Cut a portion of the quail leg and breast for each. Finish with a spoonful of sauce, and serve.

Duck Confit with Huckleberry and Potato

SERVES 4

Duck confit is one of the first dishes I learned how to cook that I truly fell in love with. When you eat fatty foods, like duck, you need to cut through the fat with acid or tartness. Huckleberries accomplish this because they are tart. Not only that, but according to at least one study, huckleberries contain almost twice as many antioxidants as blueberries. A potato terrine bridges these two ingredients so they become one balanced dish.

Ingredients

Duck confit

4 duck legs

1/2 onion

1 carrot

3 cloves of garlic

1 sprig of rosemary

1 sprig of thyme

3 cups duck fat

salt and pepper

Potato terrine

1/3 cup cream

1/4 cup vegetable stock (optional)

1/3 cup fresh horseradish, grated

1 teaspoon salt

4 large russet potatoes, sliced 1/16-inch thick

2 tablespoons fresh thyme, chopped

pepper (optional)

Instructions

How to make duck confit

You must prepare duck confit at least 1 day (preferably 2 days) in advance. On the first day, season the duck legs liberally with salt and pepper. Place them into a plastic bag and let them cure overnight. On the next day, place the duck legs into a small pot and add the onion, carrot, garlic, herbs, and duck fat. Bring the duck fat to a boil. Turn down to a very low simmer and place the lid on top. You can either cook the duck legs the rest of the way on top of the stove or you can place them into an oven at 250 degrees and leave them for about 3 hours. Cook very slowly, until the meat is about to fall off the bone. Let the duck legs cool to room temperature, then take them out of the duck fat if you plan to use them right away. Otherwise, keep the duck legs in the fat until ready to use. If the duck fat is completely covering the duck legs, they will last up to 3 months.

How to make a potato terrine

Preheat your oven to 400 degrees. In a small pot, bring the cream, vegetable stock, and horseradish to a boil. Season with 1 teaspoon of salt. Then pour the cream into a large bowl.

Next, using a mandoline, shave the potatoes into the bowl of cream. Spray a terrine dish with nonstick oil, then line the terrine with 2 large sheets of plastic wrap, allowing the edges to hang over the sides. Lay the potatoes in the terrine mold, adding a little salt and chopped thyme to each layer. Continue the process until all the potatoes are in the mold. Make sure you push the potatoes down to make them tight. I like to pour a 1/8-inch layer of excess cream over the potatoes.

continued.../

Duck Confit with Huckleberry and Potato

Huckleberry sauce

2 cups huckleberries (can be frozen)

2 cups reduced chicken stock (see page 317)

2 tablespoons garlic oil

2 tablespoons butter

8 ounces chanterelle mushrooms

salt and pepper

Garnish

nasturtium leaves

Fold the edges of the plastic wrap over the top of the potatoes. Place a cover on the terrine and bake for 80 minutes, or until a cake tester comes out clean. (You can take the lid off after about 40 minutes, if you want a little color on top of the potatoes.) Allow them to cool completely. (This works better if done a day ahead.) Using the plastic wrap as handles, remove the potatoes from the terrine and slice them into individual pieces.

How to make huckleberry sauce

Place 1 cup of huckleberries into a pot with 2 cups of reduced chicken stock. Bring to a boil, and cook for 5 minutes. Pour into a blender and purée. Season with salt, strain if desired, and pour back into your pot. Add the remaining cup of huckleberries to the sauce. Reseason, if need be, and keep on low heat until you are ready to serve.

To finish

Preheat your oven to 415 degrees. Remove as much duck fat from the duck legs as possible. In a large nonstick or cast iron skillet, place the duck legs skin-side down. Cook on medium-high heat for 4 minutes, and place the potatoes into the pan as well. Put the pan into the oven. Cook the duck legs for about 15 to 20 minutes, or until the meat and potatoes are hot all the way through. Meanwhile, in a small sauté pan, add the garlic oil, butter, and chanterelle mushrooms. Add a pinch of salt and cook for 8 minutes. Then season with more salt and pepper, if needed.

Take the duck and potatoes out of the oven. They should both be nice and crispy. Place a slice of the potato terrine on each plate. Turn the duck legs over and place them next to the potatoes. Add a few granules of sea salt on top. Add a few chanterelle mushrooms to the plate, and finish with a good helping of huckleberry sauce. Garnish with nasturtium leaves.

Duck Prosciutto

SERVES 4

Have you ever had the desire to enjoy duck prosciutto at home, but can't find it in your area. Why not make it yourself? You'll need a large mallard duck breast. (It must be large enough to withstand the curing-and-drying process when you make prosciutto.) The process is straightforward: cure the duck, dry it, and enjoy it!

Ingredients

1 large mallard duck breast

Cure mix
2 cups salt
1 1/2 cups sugar
1 sprig of thyme
1 tablespoon peppercorns
1 clove of garlic
1 teaspoon pink curing salt (optional)

Instructions

Combine all the ingredients into a bowl and mix well. Place the duck breast in either a small container or a vacuum seal bag. Pour the salt mixture all over the duck breast, making sure that it is completely covered on all sides with the cure mix. Cover the container, or seal the bag, and cure for 24 hours.

There is debate on how long to cure the duck breast. Some chefs say you need longer to cure, but the longer you cure, the more dried out your duck breast will become, creating more of a jerky than a prosciutto. When the 24 hours have passed, rinse the cure off the duck breast and pat it dry. Wrap the breast in cheese cloth, and tie a string around it. If you are able to hang the wrapped duck breast in your refrigerator, use the string to tie it to a wire rack or a door. If not, that is okay. Place the duck breast into the refrigerator and simply flip it over once every day for the next two weeks as the duck ages.

Check periodically throughout the two weeks to see whether any mold is starting to form. White mold is alright because you can cut that away, but black mold is not good and you would need to throw the meat out.

I suggest that once the two weeks have passed, you cold smoke the duck prosciutto lightly to give it another layer of flavor. (For a cold-smoking technique, see page 257.) Unwrap the duck breast from the cheese cloth. If there is any white mold, you can trim it away with a knife. You can eat the duck prosciutto at this point.

Duck Prosciutto
with Pickle and Sauce Gribiche

SERVES 4

Charcuterie is truly an art of precision and patience. This appetizer is one I created using my homemade duck prosciutto. I added pickles and radishes for acid and a bit of crunch. The pear and *sauce gribiche* took it to another level.

Ingredients

1 watermelon radish, sliced thin

1 teaspoon salt

1 pear, sliced

1/4 cup bread and butter pickles

celery leaves

Duck prosciutto

(see page 235)

Sauce gribiche

(see page 173)

Instructions

Season the watermelon radish with 1 teaspoon of salt and allow it to sit in a bowl for 5 minutes. Add a few slices of pear to the plate. Then slice the duck prosciutto very thin, and drape it over the pears. Add watermelon radish and pickles to the sliced duck. Finish with *sauce gribiche* and celery leaves.

Muscovy Duck with Eggplant and Portobello

SERVES 4

Countryside Family Farm is a local Austin farm raising a variety of animals in a natural, humane, and sustainable way. It provides most of the local restaurants and farmers markets with high quality meats. When I first prepared this dish, the owner processed the duck the day before he delivered it. You can't get much fresher than that!

Ingredients

Eggplant-potato purée
1 eggplant, peeled and diced
1 large Yukon gold potato
1 teaspoon fresh thyme, chopped
1 teaspoons fresh oregano, chopped
2 tablespoons butter
salt and pepper

Cilantro- jalapeño oil
1 large jalapeño pepper
1 small bunch of cilantro
1 clove of garlic
1 cup olive oil

Muscovy duck
2 Muscovy duck breasts, scored on the skin
2 portobello mushrooms
salt and pepper

Garnish
1 small leek, 1/8-inch thick, washed and then blanched

Instructions

For the eggplant-potato purée
Place the peeled eggplant and potato into a pot of salted water (1 teaspoon of salt, 4 cups of water). Bring to a boil, then turn down the heat and simmer for 12 to 15 minutes, or until the potatoes are cooked through. Strain off the water. Add the thyme, oregano, and butter to the eggplant and potatoes. With a hand blender or food processor, purée the vegetables until smooth. Season with salt and pepper. Set aside and keep warm.

For the duck
Remove the duck breasts from the carcasses if you happen to have the whole duck. Score the skin of the duck breast, and marinate the duck for at least 1 hour in 4 tablespoons of the cilantro-jalapeño oil. (Reserve the rest for another use.) When you are ready to cook the breasts, season the duck with salt on each side. Place the duck skin-side down into a very hot pan. Allow the duck to cook on high heat for 1 minute, then turn down the heat to medium-low for 25 to 30 minutes. (You want to render that fat down as much as possible.)

As the fat starts to accumulate in the pan, pour some of the excess into a heatproof container. About 17 minutes into the cooking process I add sliced portobello mushrooms into the pan and allow them to cook in the duck fat. Cook the mushrooms for 4 to 5 minutes on each side, and then season them with salt and pepper. Once the duck breast skin has rendered all the way down, flip the duck breast over and allow it to cook for 1 minute. Remove the duck and allow it to rest for at least 8 minutes.

To finish
Place a few spoonfuls of the eggplant-potato purée onto each plate. Add a few slices of the portobello mushrooms onto the plates. Slice the duck breast, placing the slices next to the eggplant-potato purée. Finish with some slices of blanched leek.

Wood-Roasted Duck, Apricot, and Harissa

SERVES 4

This roasted duck is alive with the flavors of North Africa. The sweetness of the apricots and the earthiness of the spices create the perfect foil for the fatty richness of the duck. I recommend cooking the breast to medium rare, but the legs should be closer to well done.

Ingredients

Apricots
2 tablespoons olive oil
3 apricots, cut in half and grilled

Harissa cheese
2 tablespoons harissa paste
4 ounces fresh sheep's milk ricotta cheese

Duck
2 whole ducks, breast still on the carcass, legs deboned, and innards reserved
2 tablespoons olive oil

Harissa spice
2 tablespoons cumin seed
3 tablespoons coriander seed
1 teaspoon caraway seed
1 tablespoon chili flakes
2 tablespoons fresh parsley (1 tablespoon, if dried)
1 tablespoon fresh garlic, minced
salt

Potatoes
1 pound yellow baby potatoes
5 tablespoons olive oil
salt and pepper

1 tablespoon butter
1 bunch heirloom spigarello broccoli greens
salt and pepper

Instructions

How to grill apricots
Drizzle 2 tablespoons of olive oil over the apricots lightly, and then grill for 1 to 2 minutes, or until nice grill marks appear on the apricots. Take them out and set them aside. (This can be done *à la minute*.)

How to make harissa cheese
Place the harissa paste and cheese into a small bowl. Mix well and set aside.

How to cook duck
I debone the legs of the duck and cut away the "tail" of the backbone with scissors, leaving the breasts still on the bone, but not on the whole carcass. Toast the spices and grind them coarsely in a spice grinder. Mix with the garlic and rub the mixture all over the duck breasts and legs. Season the duck aggressively with salt, then place the duck into a Big Green Egg or other grill set at 300 to 325 degrees. Place the duck legs skin-side down. Place the duck breast – on the bone – skin-side up. Let the duck cook for about 15 minutes, and then turn the duck breast so that it is skin-side down.

You want the skin of the duck breast to be crisp, but without the meat being completely cooked. To do this, the temperature must be hot enough to render the fat, but not so hot that you burn the skin of the duck. (If your grill is too hot, you will burn the skin of the duck. If it is too low, you won't render the skin down. I have found that a temperature range of 300 to 350 degrees is probably close to what you need.) Let the breast cook for about 15 to 20 minutes. This should really start to brown your duck breast and crisp the skin lightly. You might need to flip the legs over by this time, if they are looking golden brown and crispy. If not, keep them on the skin side. If the duck breast looks brown, take it off the grill and let it rest on a sheet pan for 15 to 20 minutes.

continued.../

Wood-Roasted Duck, Apricot, and Harissa

The meat should still be raw at this point. Place the duck breast back onto the grill skin-side down. Let it really brown, and crisp the skin, for another 15 minutes, or so. At this point the duck breast is probably getting to that medium-rare stage. Take it off the grill again. If you have a meat thermometer, you can test the internal temperature. Try to take it to the 120-degree range. When you take the breast off the grill, it will probably rise another 5 degrees, which would take you to 125 degrees.

How to roast potatoes

Preheat the oven to 400 degrees. Put the potatoes into the roasting pan. Drizzle the potatoes with olive oil, and season them with salt and pepper. Place the pan into the oven and cook for 25 minutes, or until the potatoes are just done. Take them out and let them cool to room temperature.

How to grill duck

Before you are ready to serve your duck breast (not shown in the plated picture on page 240), you'll have to place it back on the grill for 7 minutes to heat it and to give it that last little sear, or you'll have to place it into an oven at 400 degrees for 7 minutes. This should keep your duck's internal temperature between 125 and 130 degrees, which is medium-rare to medium. For the legs, the total time you want to cook them is 45 minutes to 1 hour, or until the meat is tender all the way through and the skin is crisp. The internal temperature should be around 160 degrees.

Drizzle 2 tablespoons of olive oil over the liver, gizzards, and heart, if desired, and then season them with salt and pepper. Place them onto the grill. Cook for 3 minutes, and then flip them over to cook for another 3 to 4 minutes.

Meanwhile, in a small sauté pan, add 1 tablespoon of butter with the spigarello greens. Cook for 3 minutes, then add 1/4 cup of water. Cook for another 5 minutes, or until there is no more water. Place the apricots, harissa cheese, and potatoes onto each plate. Cut the meat from the duck legs and carve it into 2 to 3 slices. Place slices onto each plate, together with a piece of the grilled liver. Add a slice of the breast (not shown in the picture) and the spigarello onto the plate.

Stuffed Shallots with Chicken, Peas, and Kimchi Broth

SERVES 6

Here is a recipe highlighting fresh peas and onions. I stuff the shallots with a chicken-dumpling mixture that I also use for pot stickers. The broth is a spicy ramen one, but you can also substitute a good chicken stock mixed with kimchi paste. This is a satisfying dish that hits a lot of umami notes.

Ingredients

Chicken filling

3 tablespoons sesame oil

1/3 cup onion, small-diced

1 tablespoon garlic, minced

1 tablespoon ginger, minced

1 whole jalapeño pepper, small-diced

4 tablespoons tamari

1 1/2 pounds chicken (ground or whole)

1 tablespoon sambal

1 tablespoon sriracha

1/2 teaspoon salt

1/4 cup cilantro leaves, chopped

1/4 cup green onion, chopped

Shallots

12 large shallots

3 tablespoons olive oil (for the finish)

salt

Instructions

For the chicken filling

In a small sauté pan on medium-high heat, add 2 tablespoons sesame oil and the diced onions, garlic, ginger, and jalapeño pepper. Cook for 5 minutes, and then add 2 tablespoons of tamari. Cook for 1 more minute, and then turn off the heat. Allow the vegetables to cool to room temperature.

Place your chicken (ground or whole) into a food processor. Purée the chicken for 20 seconds, then add the cooked-and-cooled vegetables into the food processor. Add the rest of the tamari, together with the sambal, sriracha, salt, chopped cilantro, and green onions. Purée everything together for 20 to 30 seconds, or until well combined. Test the stuffing to make sure it tastes good.

Wipe or clean the same small sauté pan you used for the vegetables, and place it on medium-high heat. Put 1 tablespoon of sesame oil into the pan. Add 1 spoonful of the chicken mixture into the pan, cooking it for 2 to 3 minutes on each side. Once it has cooked, taste the mixture and adjust the seasoning, if need be, and then refrigerate it until you are ready to use it.

For the shallots

Peel the outer layer of the shallots. In a pot of boiling, salted water (1 tablespoon of salt, 4 cups of water), blanch the whole shallots for 4 minutes. Strain out the water and place the shallots into an ice bath to stop the cooking. Once they have cooled, remove them from the ice water and dry them completely. Next, carefully remove the inner 2 to 3 layers of each shallot. You should be left with 2 outer layers of each.

continued.../

Stuffed Shallots with Chicken, Peas, and Kimchi Broth

Peas
3 cups fresh English peas, blanched
3 tablespoons butter (for the finish)

Kimchi ramen broth
3 cups chicken ramen broth
(see page 331)
2 tablespoons kimchi paste
(store-bought)
salt

Garnish
petite sorrel leaves

To stuff the shallots, you can either place your chicken filling into a plastic pastry bag or just use a spoon. Stuff all 12 shallots full of the chicken filling. (Feel free to use any remaining chicken filling for pot-stickers or an Asian chicken burger.)

For the peas
Place a pot of salted water onto the stove. Bring to a boil. Put the English peas into the water, allowing them to cook for 45 seconds to 1 minute. (Fresh peas will start to make a popping noise. This noise is usually a great indicator, letting you know that you should immediately strain out the water.) Place the peas into an ice water bath to stop the cooking process. Once they have cooled completely, strain off the peas and set them aside in a bowl.

For the kimchi ramen broth
Place 3 cups of ramen broth with 2 tablespoons of spicy kimchi paste (store-bought) into a pot. (If you don't have ramen broth, use chicken stock.) Bring to a boil and add seasoning, if need be. Set the kimchi ramen broth aside, and keep it warm.

To finish
In a large sauté pan, place all the stuffed shallots. Drizzle with olive oil and add a sprinkle of salt to each shallot. Place the shallots into an oven preheated to 400 degrees, cooking them for 20 to 22 minutes, or until the onions are tender all the way through and the chicken stuffing is cooked through.

In another sauté pan, add the ramen broth and all the blanched peas. Bring to a boil, and then add 3 tablespoons of butter. Add salt, if need be.

Ladle a few spoonfuls of the peas, with the broth, into each of 6 individual bowls. Remove the onions from the oven and place two into the middle of each bowl. Add a touch more kimchi ramen broth on top of everything. Garnish with petite sorrel leaves.

To Ski or Not To Ski

Wolfgang Puck, in my estimation, is *the* celebrity chef, *the* essence of culinary stardom. He currently owns 70 restaurants, ranging from fine food to fast food as well as many other companies.

Meeting Wolfgang

My first encounter with Chef Puck was early in my career. I was working at a Dallas hotel that hosted a celebrity chef luncheon. As I was slicing prime rib at the buffet table, Wolfgang came down the line. All I could think to say was, "Would you like some prime rib?"

My second meeting with him was more substantial, and a little more nerve-wracking. The setting was in the mountains on a beautiful snowy day. Wolfgang had tentatively committed to coming the following afternoon for hors d'oeuvres. I bought and prepped a few things for the next day.

The next morning we still didn't have confirmation that Wolfgang was coming. Since I was prepped and my love for snowboarding kicked in, I decided to go for a few runs on the mountain. Hours later I got a text, while I was on the slopes, that Wolfgang would be arriving that afternoon.

Pressure is on

There are few chefs who wouldn't feel a little bit intimidated to cook for Chef Puck. After Wolfgang arrived and introductions had been made, I got busy making appetizers. One of the appetizers I decided to serve was potato and caviar. Instead of just baking the potato and adding caviar and crème fraîche, I decided to go a bit further. I prepared the potato by cooking it sous vide with truffle and butter. Next, I breaded and fried it so it would melt in the mouth.

Because caviar is salty, I intentionally used less salt than I normally would have. In hindsight, I should have seasoned the potato a touch more, but thankfully no one seemed to notice. The right amount of seasoning can be the difference between a good bite and a great bite!

I also served Thai green curry quail (see page 229), adding a mango salsa, that was a huge hit! Homemade truffle fettuccine with fresh grated truffles was the final bite. I served this appetizer twirled around a fork, finished with Parmesan cheese, so everyone could just grab a fork and have one perfect bit of pasta.

All's well in the end

Wolfgang invited us to Spago, one of his restaurants, so that evening we all enjoyed a fantastic dinner with him. It was really special for me to have cooked for Chef Puck in the afternoon, and then to enjoy the evening with him cooking for all of us!

Veal Tenderloin with Parsnip, Morels, Cherries, and Fava Beans

SERVES 4

Veal tenderloin is one of the priciest cuts of meat, but also one of the most underrated ones. Every so often we simply have to indulge in a rich, delicious meal. The sweet cherries and morels complement this dish perfectly.

Ingredients

Parsnip purée

4 large parsnips, peeled and chopped
1 potato, peeled and chopped
3 tablespoons milk (if needed)
3 tablespoons butter
salt and pepper

Veal

1 1/2 pounds veal tenderloin
3 tablespoons olive oil
1 tablespoon rosemary, chopped
1 tablespoon parsley
1/3 cup cherries, pitted
2 tablespoons butter
salt and pepper

Vegetables

2 tablespoons olive oil
1 whole onion, sliced
1 clove of garlic
1 cup morel mushrooms, washed
1 cup fava beans, blanched and peeled
2 tablespoons water or chicken stock
1 tablespoon chopped thyme
2 tablespoons butter
salt and pepper

Instructions

For the parsnip purée

Place the chopped parsnips and potato into a pot and fill it with water. Add salt, bring to a simmer, and cook for about 25 minutes, or until both the parsnips and potatoes are cooked through. Strain off the water, and then purée with a hand blender or a ricer. Add the milk, butter, salt, and pepper to the purée. The consistency should be like a creamy mashed potato. Keep warm and set aside.

How to cook veal

Drizzle the tenderloin with olive oil, and season it with salt, pepper, chopped rosemary, and parsley. Then in a large sauté pan on medium-high heat, add the olive oil and the veal. Cook the meat for 1 minute, and then flip it. (This technique of continual flipping is called a reverse sear, as explained on page 212.) Continue flipping every minute for 8 to 9 minutes, or until you have an internal temperature of 125 degrees according to a meat thermometer. Take the veal out of the pan and allow it to rest for at least 5 minutes. Add the cherries to the pan, cooking them for 2 minutes, and then deglaze them with sherry wine. Finish with butter. The juices from the meat and the cherries should make enough for a "pan sauce."

For the vegetables

In a large sauté pan add the olive oil, onion, garlic, morel mushrooms, and a pinch of salt. Cook for 7 minutes and then add the fava beans and 2 tablespoons of water or stock. Cook for 3 minutes, then season with salt, pepper, thyme, and butter.

To finish

Put some parsnip purée onto each plate, and then add the vegetables to one side of the purée. Slice the veal and place it next to the vegetables. Spoon the cherries over the veal and the pan sauce around it.

Smoked Short Ribs with Zucchini Kimchi and Poblano-Nasturtium Sauce

SERVES 4

This recipe takes advantage of the produce you find during the hot summer months – peppers, zucchini, and nasturtiums. Typically, short ribs are paired with something hearty, like polenta or mashed potatoes. I wanted to use something lighter and less expected.

Ingredients

Marinade

2 1/2 pounds short ribs, cut into 8-ounce blocks
1 stalk lemongrass
1 finger ginger, sliced
6 cloves of garlic, chopped
1 onion, chopped
2 tablespoons sambal
1 cup orange juice
1/4 cup miso
1/2 cup tamari sauce
3 tablespoons sesame oil

Yellow zucchini squash kimchi

3 yellow zucchini squash, shaved 1/16-inch to 1/8-inch thick
2 tablespoons Korean chili flakes
1 teaspoon salt

Instructions

For the short rib

Heat your Big Green Egg or grill to 275 to 300 degrees. Place the short ribs into a ziplock bag. Add all the ingredients into a blender to make the marinade. Purée for 30 seconds. Pour the marinade over the short ribs, allowing them to marinate for 1 or 2 hours.

If you don't have a roasting pan you want to put on the grill, make a little boat with 2 to 3 sheets of aluminum foil. Place the short ribs inside the aluminum "boat" and pour the marinade over them. Place the short ribs into your Big Green Egg, basting them every 45 minutes. If you need to add a little water to the marinade because it is evaporating, do so. Cook for 4 to 5 hours, or until the short ribs are completely tender all the way through.

How to make kimchi

In a bowl add your zucchini squash and the rest of the ingredients, mixing them together for 2 minutes. Make sure everything is completely and thoroughly mixed. Pack the mixture into a 1-quart jar, making sure everything is inside the jar. The liquid must completely cover the vegetables, and you need to leave about 1 inch of free space at the top of the jar. (If you have a weight, you can place a small piece of parchment paper on top of the vegetables, and then place that weight on top of the parchment paper. The weight will ensure that the vegetables stay below the surface of the liquid.)

Place the lid on top of the kimchi jar and allow the kimchi to ferment for at least 7 days. You should "burp" the jar every other day because pressure builds up during the fermentation process, so some of the gases need to be released. The longer you allow the kimchi to ferment, the more intense the flavor will be. If you want to bypass the fermentation, do the same process, allowing the kimchi to marinate for at least 1 to 2 hours before using it.

continued.../

Smoked Short Ribs with Zucchini Kimchi and Poblano-Nasturtium Sauce

Vegetables

2 Yukon potatoes

4 tablespoons olive oil

1/2 onion, diced

1 avocado, diced

2 apriums, diced

Poblano-nasturtium sauce

(see page 315)

Garnish

2 tablespoons chives, chopped

2 tablespoons sesame seeds, toasted

1 tablespoon chive blossoms

To finish

Place the potatoes into the microwave for 4 minutes. Take them out, allowing them to cool slightly. Small dice the potatoes, and then place them into a sauté pan at medium heat with 4 tablespoons of olive oil. Cook for 3 minutes, then add the onion. Cook for another 4 minutes, and season with salt and pepper. Add the diced avocado and apriums to the pan, then turn off the heat.

Place a spoonful of the poblano-nasturtium sauce onto each plate. Put a ring mold on top of the sauce, and spoon the potato mixture into the ring mold, gently patting it down. Baste the short ribs with the juices, and then place them on top of the potato mixture. Add the zucchini kimchi next to the short ribs. Garnish with chives, sesame seeds, and chive blossoms.

Beef Carpaccio

SERVES 4

Beef carpaccio is one my favorite simple dishes to eat. Carpaccio basically means thinly sliced raw meat or fish. This recipe is a quick version using beef tenderloin. In the restaurant business, chefs will often tie the tenderloin or strip steak before freezing it into a cylindrical shape. Once the meat is frozen, a chef will use an electric slicer to shave paper-thin slices off. Since I don't have an industrial meat slicer, I improvise a bit. The best way I know to achieve the same result is to sear the beef very slightly on each side, then to cut the fillet into thin slices. Using a mallet, pound the slices paper thin. Finish the carpaccio with classic garnishes, like capers, Parmesan cheese, and aioli sauce.

Ingredients

Parmesan crisps
1 cup Parmesan cheese, shredded

Beef carpaccio
12 ounces beef tenderloin, cut into 2 even steaks (6 ounces each)
3 tablespoons olive oil

Mustard aioli sauce
1/2 cup Vegenaise or mayonnaise
2 tablespoons whole grain mustard
salt

Salad
1/4 cup fennel, shaved paper thin
2 whole red radishes, julienned
1/4 cup celery leaves (preferably the hearts)
1/4 cup chervil (or parsley)
1/2 whole lemon (for juice)
3 tablespoons olive oil
salt and pepper

Garnish
1 ounce Parmesan cheese, shaved
1/4 cup capers
3 tablespoons green onion, chopped

Instructions

How to make Parmesan crisps
Preheat the oven to 400 degrees. Line a sheet pan (or a silicone baking mat) with parchment paper. Place a round cookie cutter (as big or as small as you like) at one corner of the sheet pan. Put a small handful of shredded Parmesan cheese into the mold, creating one smooth layer of cheese (about 1/8-inch thick – not a mound of cheese). Repeat the process, moving the ring over and leaving about 1 inch between piles. You should be able to cook 6 to 8 Parmesan crisps on a half sheet pan.

Remove the ring mold, place the sheet pan into the oven, and cook for 8 to 10 minutes, or until the crisps are golden brown. Take them out, allow them to cool, and then transfer them to a paper towel to drain any excess oil. Once cooled, they should be crunchy like crackers. Set them aside until you are ready to use them, or place them into an airtight container for later use.

For the beef carpaccio
Season both beef steaks heavily with 1 tablespoon of olive oil, salt, and pepper. Sear the steaks quickly (about 1 minute on each side) on all sides in a hot pan. Take the steaks out and allow them to cool completely.

continued.../

Beef Carpaccio

Place a piece of plastic wrap on the countertop. With a sharp knife, slice the steak to make thin slices and place them on top of the plastic wrap. Cover the slices with another piece of plastic. The meat slices should be sandwiched between two sheets of plastic. With a mallet, lightly tap the meat slices to flatten them paper thin, but without tearing the meat. Remove all the plastic, then place the slices of meat onto a plate. I use a large round cookie cutter to make a perfect circle. This can be done ahead of time, so you can wrap each individual plate and refrigerate until time to serve. The slicing and refrigerating should be done in advance for a party.

To finish

In a bowl, mix the Vegenaise (or mayonnaise) and mustard with salt, and then put the mixture into a squeeze bottle. Uncover the meat, and squirt dots of the mustard aioli sauce over the top. In another bowl, create a salad with the fennel, radish, celery leaves, and chervil. Season them with lemon juice, olive oil, salt, and pepper. Line the greens over the meat, and top them with shaved Parmesan cheese and one Parmesan crisp. Finish the plate with a drizzle of the remaining olive oil. Add the capers, green onions, and
a little sea salt.

Smoked A5 Kobe Rib Eye with Farro, Gochujang, and Endive

SERVES 4

With prized beef like A5 Kobe, I never want to overpower its natural flavor. Cold smoking is one of my go-to secrets that really boosts the flavor of a protein without it being marinated. Because of the high level of fat content in the steak, I don't want the other ingredients to be heavy. I add Korean gochujang for spice, grains for substance, and endive to finish the dish.

Ingredients

2 A5 Kobe rib eyes, 1 pound each
2 tablespoons olive oil
salt and pepper

Grains

1 cup farro
5 cups water
1 teaspoon salt (for water to cook the farro)
1 cup lentils, cooked (see page 57)
1 cup urad gota, cooked (see page 163)
3/4 cup spring onions, chopped
2 tablespoons soy sauce
2 tablespoons butter
salt and pepper

Vegetables

3 spring onion bulbs, cut in half
2 Belgium endives, cut in quarters

Instructions

For the ribeyes

Put applewood and pecan wood chips into the bottom of your stove-top smoker. Place the grate over the wood chips, and the tray on top of the grate. Then place ice into a ziplock bag, or use ice blocks, wrapping them with foil. Put the ice on top of the tray. Place the rib eye steaks on top of the ice bag or ice block on top of the tray. The cover probably won't fit on top of your stove-top smoker. If that's the case, you can cover the smoker with aluminum foil. Turn on the heat so the chips will start smoking. Allow the heat to stay on a maximum of 1 to 2 minutes once you see the smoke coming out of the smoker. Turn off the heat, but keep the rib eyes inside the smoker for another 20 to 30 minutes. The ice will keep the steaks raw while they are infused with smoke.

For the farro

Rinse the farro under cold water. Add 5 cups of water and 1 teaspoon of salt to a sauce pot. Bring to a boil, and then pour in your farro. Cover, and then turn down to a simmer. Simmer for about 35 to 45 minutes, or until the farro is tender. Strain off any excess water, reserving it for later. Put the farro onto a sheet pan, spreading it evenly, and allow it to cool.

For the grain compote

In a small pot add the cooked farro, lentils, urad gota, and onions, together with 1/4 cup of the liquid reserved after cooking the farro. Add the soy sauce and cook for 5 minutes to heat up the mixture. Add the butter, and then season with salt and pepper. Set the grain compote aside and keep it warm.

continued.../

Smoked A5 Kobe Rib Eye with Farro, Gochujang, and Endive

Gochujang aioli

(see page 315)

Garnish

purslane

To finish

Remove your rib eyes from the smoker and season them with salt and pepper aggressively. In a large, medium-hot sauté pan with 2 tablespoons of olive oil, add the rib eyes and cook for 1 1/2 minutes. Flip the steaks and cook for another 1 1/2 minutes. Flip them again, repeating the process 4 to 5 more times. The rib eyes should be close to medium rare. (This technique of continual flipping is called a reverse sear, as explained on page 212.) With the A5 being so fatty, you can go another 1 or 2 minutes. It is okay to cook to a medium because the steaks will be extremely moist and tender.

Add the onion bulbs around the steaks. Take the rib eyes off the heat and allow them to rest for at least 5 to 10 minutes. While the steaks are resting, add the endive to the pan with the onions, and cook for 4 to 5 minutes. Season with salt and pepper. The fat from the steaks will give extra flavor to both the onions and the endive.

If the steaks have cooled down too much, you can place them back into the pan for another 1 or 2 minutes to warm them up. Meanwhile, place a spoonful of gochujang aioli sauce onto each plate, and then add the lentil-farro mixture into a ring mold on top of the sauce. Using the back of the spoon, press down on the mixture to make sure it is tightly bound inside the ring mold. Place the onion bulb halves on top of the lentil-farro mixture, and then one endive on top of the onions. Add 5 slices of rib eye for each plate, arranging them around the lentil mixture. Add purslane and serve.

Venison Rack with Kabocha and Molasses Pepper Glaze

SERVES 4

When fall arrives it's time for wild game. This dish is perfect for the grill or a smoker. I include a few basic ingredients that add a lot of flavor with minimal effort. Venison has a strong, distinctive taste, and it pairs well with the kabocha and the molasses pepper glaze in this recipe. You won't find many dishes as quick-and-easy as this one.

Ingredients

1 kabocha squash
2 tablespoons olive oil

Molasses pepper glaze
1 cup dark molasses
(I prefer Grandma's® Molasses)
2 tablespoons whole grain
Dijon mustard
4 tablespoons fresh black pepper,
course-ground

Venison
1 rack venison, cleaned
butcher twine
2 tablespoons olive oil
1 sprig of sage
1 sprig of thyme
salt and pepper

Instructions

For the kabocha squash

Add lump coal to your Big Green Egg or other grill and start your fire. Immediately add the kabocha squash directly to the coals, allowing it to remain there for 1 hour as your grill reaches about 400 degrees. Remove the kabocha squash from the coals, setting it on top of the grill rack while you prepare the venison.

For the molasses pepper glaze

Place all the ingredients into a bowl and whisk together well. Set the glaze aside until you are ready to use it.

For the venison rack

Using butcher's twine, tie each chop next to each bone on both sides of the chop. Drizzle the chops with 2 tablespoons of olive oil, and then season them with salt, pepper, and herbs. Place the chops directly onto the grill and cook them for about 8 minutes. Flip them over and spoon a little bit of the molasses glaze on them.

Cook for another 8 to 10 minutes, or until your meat thermometer reads 125 degrees in the middle of the rack. Remove the venison from the grill and allow it to rest for at least 5 to 10 minutes. Remove the kabocha squash as well. Cut the kabocha squash in half and scoop out the seeds. Drizzle 2 tablespoons of olive oil over the halves, season them with salt and pepper, and then cut them into quarter wedges.

continued.../

Venison Rack with Kabocha and Molasses Pepper Glaze

Vinaigrette
3 tablespoons olive oil
2 teaspoons sherry vinegar
salt and pepper

Beet salad
1 small candy-striped beet,
shaved thin, raw
1 red beet, shaved thin, raw
1 cup mâche
salt and pepper

For the vinaigrette
In a small bowl, add 3 tablespoons of olive oil and the vinegar, salt, and pepper. Mix well.

To finish
Toss the beets and mâche with the salt and pepper, as well as a little of the vinaigrette. Cut the twine from the venison and slice the meat into individual portions. Drizzle a little of the molasses glaze onto each plate. Add the kabocha, a chop, and beet salad to each plate.

We all look forward to dessert. In the beginning of my career, I didn't have a lot of opportunities to dive into the sweet side of the business, but I really fell in love with it once I had the chance. I have always had a sweet tooth and have grown to love baking with vanilla, almond paste, and citrus. Developing recipes around these ingredients has upped my dessert game while I have been developing as a chef.

Fruit is Mother Nature's naturally sweet treat. Therefore, it usually finds its way into the majority of my desserts. One way I love to use fruit is in fresh sorbets. They require just a few ingredients and will work for those who have an egg or milk allergy. I have access to all kinds of fruit trees, including mulberry, stone fruit, and sapote. They provide me with endless opportunities to make not only wonderful sorbets, but other desserts as well. In season, grocery store produce can also yield phenomenal results.

This section of my cookbook includes a variety of desserts and techniques giving you many choices for satisfying a sweet tooth. From time to time, we all need to indulge a little – so please do.

SWEETS

Banana and Hazelnut Bomb with Banana Cinnamon Ice Cream

SERVES 12

I love bananas, but like most people, I am often left with one or two bananas that turn brown and get soft before I can eat them. Instead of tossing them into the bin, I like to place mine in the freezer. Once I've accumulated a bunch, I make banana bread, sorbet, or some sort of a dessert. For this recipe, I make all three, with the addition of Nutella® and hazelnuts. I finish the dish with a caramel sauce.

Ingredients

Nutella® filling
1/2 cup Nutella®
4 ounces cream cheese
1/4 cup ground hazelnut
1 tablespoon Frangelico

Banana mousse
8 bananas, overly ripened, or frozen and thawed, and completely drained of water (peels should be black)
8 ounces mascarpone cheese
2 3/4 teaspoons gelatin
3 tablespoons water
1 1/2 cups heavy cream
1/2 cup powdered sugar
1 teaspoon vanilla
3 egg whites
1/2 cup sugar

Instructions

For the Nutella® filling
In a stand mixer with a paddle attachment, mix all the ingredients well until you have one homogenous mix. Fill a 15-cavity half-sphere mold with the mixture, then freeze it until it is completely solid.

For the banana mousse
Using a hand blender, purée your ripened bananas and mascarpone cheese until smooth. In a separate small bowl, add the gelatin and water (to bloom the gelatin). Meanwhile, in a stand mixer, using the whisk, add the heavy cream. When the cream starts to thicken, add the powdered sugar and vanilla. Whip until stiff peaks form. Place the whipped cream into a bowl and refrigerate it. Clean your mixing bowl out, then place your egg whites inside. Make a quick meringue by mixing the egg whites on high with the whisk attachment, and when the whites start to foam, slowly add 1/2 cup of sugar. Whip until you have stiff peaks.

Melt the gelatin over a double boiler, pour it into the banana mixture, and mix well. Working quickly now, fold your egg whites into the banana mixture, turning the bowl and folding. Next, fold your whipped cream in the same fashion. (You want to incorporate the whipped cream well, but you don't want to overwork it.) Fill 2 bomb molds almost to the top. Your molds should have 6 cavities of 3 ounces each.

Once you have all 12 cavities filled, remove your frozen Nutella® half-sphere mold from the freezer. Place one half sphere of the Nutella® filling into the center of each of the 12 banana mousses. Using an offset spatula, smooth out the tops of the mousses – you might need to add a touch more mousse to cover the middle of each sphere completely. Once they are completely smooth, put them into the freezer overnight to set.

continued.../

Banana and Hazelnut Bomb
with Banana Cinnamon Ice Cream

Hazelnut banana cake

3 1/4 cups all-purpose flour

1 1/2 teaspoons salt

1 teaspoon ground nutmeg

2 teaspoons baking soda

1 teaspoon ground cinnamon

3 cups sugar

1 cup vegetable oil

1 teaspoon vanilla

4 eggs, beaten

7 thawed bananas

1/3 cup banana water

1 cup hazelnut, chopped

Caramel sauce

8 ounces brown sugar

4 ounces butter

4 ounces Patrón XO Cafe

6 ounces cream

Banana cinnamon ice cream

4 egg yolks

3/4 cup sugar

1 1/2 cups milk

1 1/2 cups cream

4 ripe frozen bananas, thawed

1 teaspoon cinnamon

1 tablespoon vanilla extract

2 ripe bananas

sugar

1/4 cup of roasted hazelnuts,
cut in half and quarter-ground

For the hazelnut banana cake

Preheat the oven to 350 degrees. In a large bowl, combine the flour, salt, nutmeg, baking soda, cinnamon, and sugar. In a separate bowl, combine the oil, vanilla, eggs, bananas, and banana water. Mix the wet ingredients into the dry ones, and add the hazelnuts, folding them into the mixture.

Pour the cake mixture onto a half sheet pan that has been sprayed with non-stick spray. Bake for 30 to 35 minutes, or until a cake tester comes out clean. Remove the cake from the oven and allow it to cool completely. Once it has completely cooled, you can refrigerate it, if desired. Using a cookie cutter that is the same size as your bomb molds, cut out 12 cakes for your 12 bombs, then set them aside.

For the caramel sauce

Place the brown sugar and butter into a small pot and cook on medium heat until the butter has melted and the sugar has dissolved. Add the Patrón XO Café and flambé. Let all the alcohol cook off, and add the cream. Whisk until all is combined, then cook for 2 to 3 minutes, or until you have the desired thickness. Turn off the heat and set the sauce aside until you are ready to plate.

For the ice cream

Place the egg yolks into a stand mixer and set it to medium speed. Slowly pour in your sugar. Whip for about 4 minutes until the mixture is light and fluffy. Meanwhile, start the ice cream base by adding all the milk and cream to a saucepot. Bring the milk-cream mixture slowly to a boil, then turn off the heat. With a ladle, temper your egg yolks by ladling a little of the milk-cream mixture into the egg yolks, while whisking, until you have about half of the mixture left.

Banana and Hazelnut Bomb
with Banana Cinnamon Ice Cream

Pour the tempered egg yolk mixture back into the pot with the remaining milk and cream, using a spatula to scrape the sides. Turn the heat back on low. Stir for about 5 minutes, then turn off the heat. You can let the mixture cool in the refrigerator if you have the time, or place it into a bowl inside an ice bath to cool down faster. Once the mixture has cooled completely, you can add the bananas, cinnamon, and vanilla with a blender. Purée until completely smooth, and then place the mixture into your ice cream machine until it is done. Once the ice cream is finished, take it out, place it into a container, and store it in the freezer.

To finish

Place a round piece of the hazelnut banana cake onto each plate. Remove the bomb molds from the freezer and take the bombs out of the molds, placing each one on top of a piece of cake. Slice ripe bananas, and place the slices onto a sheet tray. Sprinkle the tops liberally with sugar. Using a torch, caramelize the sugar on top of the bananas. Add some ground hazelnuts next to each bomb, and add a scoop of banana ice cream on top. Spoon some of the caramel on top of each bomb and around it. Add the hazelnuts on top and around as well. Finish by placing caramelized banana slices around.

Note: To make things a little easier and to avoid having the mousse frozen too much, you can unmold the bomb and place it on top of the hazelnut banana cake, storing everything in the refrigerator until you are ready to serve dessert. This tip will help you serve everyone more quickly, and it will prevent the center of each dessert from being completely frozen in the middle.

Vanilla Crème Brûlée

SERVES 4

There are classics for a reason – they are proven to work and they are absolutely delicious! The key to a great crème brûlée is patience. You can't rush crème brûlée, which means your oven needs to be set at the right temperature. If the oven is too hot and it cooks too fast, the results will be a curdle brûlée instead of a silky, smooth custard. That is the telltale sign for distinguishing a good brûlée from a bad one. The final factor is whether the recipe calls for vanilla bean rather than extract. There is no comparison between a real vanilla bean and extract. This recipe includes only four ingredients, so use the best and be patient

Ingredients

4 egg yolks
3/4 cup sugar
1/2 vanilla bean
1 pint (16 fluid ounces) heavy whipping cream

1/4 cup sugar (for the brûlée)

Instructions

Place the egg yolks into a stand mixer with a whisk attachment. Add 3/4 cup of sugar and turn on low for 10 seconds, then turn to high for 2 to 3 minutes, or until the yolks are pale and fluffy. Meanwhile, cut the vanilla bean in half, scrape the seeds out, and place both the seeds and the pod into a pot with the cream.

Heat the cream until it just starts to boil. Temper the egg mixture with the hot cream by adding 4 ounces of cream at a time to the stand mixer while it is on low. Continue, adding the rest of the cream. This recipe makes enough for 4 large ramekins, or about 10 small cups.

Preheat your oven to 275 degrees. Pour the brûlée into your ramekins / cups, and then place them inside a deep baking dish. Add really hot water into the baking dish so that the water goes halfway up the sides of the ramekins. Cover the baking dish with foil fairly tightly, and then place it into the oven. Bake for 30 to 35 minutes. (Depending on how hot your oven truly is when set to 275 degrees, and what size ramekins you use, you might need an extra 10 minutes of baking time.) After the brûlée has baked, lift a corner of the foil covering the baking dish. (The steam can burn you, so be careful.) What you want to see when you shake the ramekins is that the brûlées are firm, but jiggle. If so, they are done.

continued…/

Vanilla Crème Brûlée

If the brûlées are runny, milky, or look like they did before you put them into the oven, they aren't done. What you don't want to see is scrambled eggs in cream! If they aren't done, just put them back into the oven for another 5 to 10 minutes, then check on them again. I've had some take 30 to 35 minutes, but others take 50 minutes. The time really depends on the oven. Once the brûlées are done, take them out and allow them to cool. Place them into the refrigerator for at least 3 hours.

To finish

Take the crème brûlées out of the refrigerator. Sprinkle a teaspoon or two of sugar on top of each ramekin, making sure to distribute the sugar evenly. Then take a blow torch and slowly caramelize the sugar on top. Be sure not to get the torch too close to the sugar. The closer you are, the hotter the flame, which means the faster the sugar can burn. You don't want burnt sugar. A golden dark brown – not black – is perfect. Continue to torch all the ramekins, caramelizing all the sugar. Wait 30 seconds, and then serve.

Berries and Cream, and Honey Cake with Crème Fraîche Ice Cream

SERVES 8–10

Who doesn't love honey? This moist cake is saturated with cinnamon, honey, and citrus. Honey cake is a Mediterranean-style cake, similar to a baklava, in that after it has baked, a honey syrup is poured over the cake and completely absorbed into it. I add my version of berries and cream to finish this amazing dessert.

Ingredients

Crème fraîche ice cream
14 1/2 ounces milk
1/2 cup sugar
1/2 cup trimoline inverted sugar
1/4 cup glucose
3 ounces cream cheese or ricotta cheese
12 ounces crème fraîche
2 teaspoons lemon juice
1 teaspoon salt

Honey syrup
1 cup honey
3/4 cup sugar
3/4 cup water
2 tablespoons lemon juice

Greek honey lavender cake
1 cup flour
1/4 cup corn starch
1 1/2 teaspoons baking powder
1/2 teaspoon salt
1/2 teaspoon cinnamon
1 tablespoon lavender, fresh-chopped
1 teaspoon lemon zest
1 1/2 sticks butter
3/4 cup sugar, plus 3 tablespoons
3 eggs
3/4 cup milk

Instructions

For the crème fraîche ice cream
In a small saucepot over medium heat, warm the milk, then add the sugar, trimoline, and glucose until they have dissolved. Pour the milk into a blender with the ricotta cheese and crème fraîche, then purée until smooth. Strain through a strainer into a bowl in an ice bath. Add the lemon juice and season with salt. Cool completely, then pour everything into your ice cream maker to freeze according to its directions. When the ice cream is done, place it into an airtight container in the freezer until you are ready to serve it.

For the honey syrup
In a saucepan, combine the honey, sugar, and water. Bring to a simmer and cook 5 minutes. Stir in the lemon juice, bring to a boil, and cook for 2 minutes.

For the Greek honey lavender cake
Preheat your oven to 350 degrees. Grease and flour a half sheet pan (13-inch-square). Combine the dry ingredients (flour, starch, baking powder, salt, cinnamon, lavender, and lemon zest). Set aside. In a large bowl, blend the butter and sugar until the mixture is light and fluffy. Beat in the eggs one at a time.

Beat the flour mixture into the milk, mixing only until it has been incorporated. Pour the batter into the prepared half sheet pan. Bake in the preheated oven for 15 to 20 minutes, or until a toothpick inserted into the center of the cake comes out clean. Allow to cool for 10 minutes, and then cut the cake into desired shapes. Pour your honey syrup over the cake.

continued.../

Berries and Cream, and Honey Cake
with Crème Fraîche Ice Cream

Strawberry coulis

1/3 cup white wine or champagne

1 pound strawberries, cut in half

1/3 cup sugar

5 sprigs of fresh chamomile

1 cup small strawberries

1 cup blueberries

1/2 cup cherries, halved

1/3 cup wild strawberries
(Alpine, or Fragaria vesca)

1 Snow Princess flower

3 chamomile flowers

1/4 cup red veined sorrel leaves

For the strawberry coulis

In a small pot, combine all the ingredients, except for the chamomile, and bring to a boil. Turn down and simmer for 10 minutes. Purée until smooth. Add the chamomile and let it steep for 10 minutes, then discard the chamomile. Place the coulis into the refrigerator until it is completely cold.

To finish

Add a few pieces of cake around the middle of each plate. Add the strawberries, blueberries, and cherries in an alternating pattern between pieces of cake. Add some wild strawberries on top of the honey cake. Add the flowers and herbs for garnishes. Ladle some of the coulis into the middle of the plate. Finish with a scoop of the crème fraîche ice cream.

Mulberry Tart with Jam, Pastry Cream, and Whipped Cream

SERVES 8–10

Mulberries signal the beginning of summer. We have two varieties growing on the California property. One is a huge tree. Its mulberries resemble blackberries, but with a difference. Little hair-like spurs grow out of the mulberries. They start off white, gradually changing color to red, and continue changing color until they finally end up dark purple, which indicates that the mulberry has fully ripened.

The other variety is more like a vine or bush (the ever-bearing mulberry tree). I find this tree so interesting because the leaves not only protect it from sunlight all day long, but they can actually catch the berries when they drop. This recipe calls for mulberry jam stuffed inside a tart with pastry cream, and topped with vanilla whipped cream.

Ingredients

Pastry cream

2 cups milk

1 vanilla bean

4 egg yolks

3/4 cup sugar

1/4 cup cornstarch

2 tablespoons butter

Tart crust

2 cups flour to start, plus an additional 3 tablespoons, if needed

1 teaspoon salt

1 1/2 sticks butter

1/4 cup ice water

1 egg yolk

Instructions

How to make pastry cream

For the pastry cream, scald the milk and vanilla bean in a medium saucepot. Turn off the heat when the milk starts to boil. Meanwhile, beat the egg yolks and sugar in a bowl until the eggs and sugar form pale white ribbons. This should take about 2 minutes. Add the cornstarch to the eggs and sugar, and beat for another 30 seconds. Temper the egg mixture by whisking in one ladle of milk at a time until all the milk is incorporated. Place the egg mixture back into the pot on low heat and whisk continually to thicken the pudding. Allow about 10 minutes on medium low. Once the mixture has thickened, add the butter and whisk until it is completely incorporated. Pour the pastry cream into a bowl. (You can pour it through a strainer, if desired.)

Place a piece of plastic wrap on the surface of the pastry cream so it doesn't form a skin, and place the bowl into the refrigerator. Leave the vanilla bean in the pudding until everything has cooled, and then discard the bean.

How to make tart crust

Using a food processor, add 2 cups of flour to a bowl along with the salt. Pulse a few times to combine well, and add all the butter at one time. Turn the processor on and let it blend the ingredients for 20 seconds. Once the butter has been combined with the flour, drizzle in the cold water and egg yolk. Finish with a few tablespoons of flour, if needed.

continued.../

Mulberry Tart with Jam, Pastry Cream, and Whipped Cream

**Mulberry jam
(small batch with pectin)**

2 cups mulberries

2 lemons, juiced

2 tablespoons water

3/4 cup sugar

1/2 vanilla bean or
1 tablespoon vanilla bean paste

1 teaspoon pectin

whipped cream (see page 318)

fresh mulberries

edible flowers

Carefully place your tart dough inside your tart mold, or molds. (I prefer 6 small tartlet molds, using half of the tart recipe.) Press the tart dough into all the corners of the mold(s). Use a rolling pin to press the dough down, and then trim off any excess hanging over the sides. Cut a piece of parchment paper so that it fits your tart exactly. Use pie weights or dried beans to fill the inside of the tart and parchment paper. Preheat an oven to 400 degrees, then place the tart crust inside for 18 minutes. Take it out and set it aside. Once it has cooled, add 1 1/2 tablespoons of pastry cream to the bottom of each tart.

For the mulberry jam

In a medium-sized pot, add the mulberries, lemon juice, water, sugar, and vanilla bean. As the berries start to simmer, crush them with a masher or a hand stick blender until they are almost smooth. (I like little bits of berries in my jam, so I don't purée it until it is totally smooth.) Bring to a boil and cook for 4 to 5 minutes, then stir in the pectin powder. Stir continually for another 1 or 2 minutes, and turn off the heat. You can simply allow the jam to cool a bit – for 10 to 15 minutes – and then fill your tarts. Cool completely.

Pour 1 or 2 spoonfuls of jam into each tart shell on top of the pastry cream. Place the tarts into the refrigerator to cool for at least 2 hours. (Or if you want to preserve the jam, fill an 8-ounce jar, seal it tightly, and flip it over. Allow it to stay like that until it has come to room temperature and the top has popped.)

To finish

Put the whipped cream into a piping bag and create little dots on the tarts. Add some fresh mulberries to the top with any edible flowers you desire.

Lemon Meringue Tart

SERVES 6–8

Lemon meringue tart is another classic dessert, and it takes advantage of lemons in season. Typically, you can harvest once in the summer and once in the winter. This dessert is the perfect balance between sweet and tart. The meringue, one that could be mistaken as marshmallow, finishes the tart in a refined fashion.

Ingredients

Tart crust (pâte brisée)

2 cups flour, plus 3 tablespoons, if needed

1 teaspoon salt

2 sticks butter

1/4 cup ice water

Lemon curd

1/2 cup lemon juice

2 teaspoons zest

1/2 cup sugar

3 eggs

1 stick butter

Swiss meringue

1/2 cup egg whites

3/4 cup sugar

Instructions

How to make the tart crust

Using a food processor, add 2 cups of flour and 1 teaspoon of salt. Pulse a few times to combine well. Then add all the butter at one time. Turn the processor on and let it run for 20 seconds. Once the butter has been combined into the mixture, drizzle in the cold water. Finish with a few tablespoons of flour, if needed.

Usually you would put the crust into the refrigerator at this stage to let the dough come together as it becomes colder. However, I don't like my dough to be so cold that I can't roll it, and I am often in a rush. Putting the dough into the freezer for 15 minutes will really help, but if that is not possible, simply put a light dusting of flour onto parchment paper and place the dough on top. Then dust flour on top of the dough, placing a second piece of parchment paper over the dough. With a rolling pin, roll out your dough to a thin-crust consistency. Carefully place your tart dough inside a tart mold. (You can make one large tart or about 7 small ones. I like to use half the tart dough for this recipe, making 7 small tarts in small tart rings.)

Use a rolling pin to press the dough down, then trim off any excess hanging over the sides. Cut a piece of parchment paper so that it fits your tart exactly. Use pie weights or dried beans to fill the inside of the tart and parchment paper. Preheat an oven to 400 degrees, and then place the tart crust inside for 18 minutes. Take it out and set it aside.

continued.../

Lemon Meringue Tart

For the lemon curd

Place all the ingredients into a small saucepot and turn on medium-low heat, whisking continually until the curd starts to thicken. This should take about 10 minutes. Once it has thickened, strain the mixture into a bowl and place it into the refrigerator to cool down. After it is completely cool, you can fill each tart shell – if you used small ones – or one big tart shell 1/2 to 3/4 of the way full of curd. Place the tart(s) back into the refrigerator until you are ready for your meringue.

For the Swiss meringue

In a mixing bowl, heat the egg whites and sugar over a water bath, stirring frequently with a whisk, until they reach 160 degrees. Immediately place them into a stand mixer with the whisk attachment. Whip for 5 minutes, or until the meringue is cool. Put it into a pastry bag with a plain tip. Set aside.

To finish

Pipe little dollops of meringue all over your tart(s). Using a torch (if you have one) or your broiler, toast the meringue quickly.

Strawberry Parfait with Sorbet and Shortbread

SERVES 12

Memories of eating strawberry shortcake ice cream bars in childhood was my inspiration for this dessert when I first made it. I wanted to make a modern version of this classic dessert bar, but I admit that this recipe is a liberal interpretation. The final product was actually an amazing light and refreshing dessert. This French-style parfait uses gelatin, whipped cream, and coconut milk, which added another layer of subtle but sweet flavor.

Ingredients

Strawberry parfait

1 can coconut milk

3 cups whole strawberries

3/4 cup granulated sugar

2 1/2 teaspoons beef gelatin powder

3 tablespoons water

1 1/4 cups heavy cream

1/4 cup confectioners' sugar

1 teaspoon vanilla

Shortbread

1 cup butter, softened

1/2 cup sugar, plus 2 tablespoons for sprinkling dough

1 teaspoon salt

2 1/2 cups flour

strawberry sorbet

2 1/3 cups water

2 cups sugar

4 cups whole strawberries

1 large lemon, juiced

1/2 cup fresh strawberries, sliced

micro sorrel

Instructions

How to make strawberry parfait

Prepare an ice bath in a large bowl. Place your coconut milk and strawberries into a blender, and purée until smooth. Pour into a pot, turn on the heat, and add the granulated sugar. Stir until the sugar has dissolved and the mixture is hot. Meanwhile, in a separate, small bowl, add the gelatin and 3 tablespoons of water to bloom.

Turn the heat off the strawberry-coconut mixture. Add a little of it to the gelatin, and with a whisk, mix well to dissolve the gelatin. Then pour the rest of the gelatin mixture and the strawberry-coconut mixture into a bowl. Set the bowl into an ice bath. Stir the mixture for a few minutes as it cools down. Meanwhile, in a stand mixer, add the heavy cream, and using a whisk, whip it.

When the cream starts to thicken, add the confectioners' sugar and the vanilla. Whip until you see stiff peaks. Then, when the strawberry mixture has cooled but not gelled, gently whisk in the whipped cream. You want to incorporate the whipped cream, but without overworking it. Once you have combined it, pour the mixture onto a half sheet pan and place it into the freezer for at least 2 hours.

continued.../

Strawberry Parfait with Sorbet and Shortbread

How to make shortbread

Using an electric mixer, beat your butter until it is soft and fluffy. This should take about 1 1/2 minutes. Add the granulated sugar and salt, and mix well. Next, add the flour in 3 stages, and mix until just blended. Remove the dough and roll it so that it is 1/4-inch thick. Place the dough onto a sheet pan lined with parchment paper, sprinkle with 2 tablespoons of sugar, and bake it at 375 degrees for roughly 18 minutes, or until it is golden brown. Then, after it cools completely, take half of the shortbread and place it into a food processor, pulsing until it is coarse. (If you prefer, you can place the shortbread into a plastic bag, and crush it with a mallet.) Set the shortbread aside until you are ready to plate.

How to make strawberry sorbet

Place the water and sugar into a pot. Bring the pot to a boil, cooking for 5 minutes. Cool it slightly, then place the mixture into a blender with the whole strawberries. Purée until smooth, and add the lemon juice. Chill the mixture until it is completely cold. Place it into an ice cream maker, and follow the machine's instructions. When the sorbet is done, place it into the freezer in an airtight container.

To finish

In a bowl, using a ring mold, add the coarse-ground shortbread. Take the parfait out of the freezer, cutting it with a ring cutter and placing the parfait on top of the shortbread. Add a scoop of sorbet to each dish, and then add the fresh sliced strawberries to the parfait. Finish with micro sorrel.

Persimmon and Orange Rum Baba

SERVES 8

Although rum baba originated in France, people enjoy variations of this small yeast cake in many parts of the world. When I developed this recipe, I was looking for something different to make with persimmons, my favorite winter fruit. I decided to incorporate them into baba dough. The addition of sabayon and orange is the perfect finish.

Ingredients

Baba dough
2/3 cup milk
2 1/2 packets yeast
3 1/3 cups flour
4 tablespoons sugar
1 teaspoon salt
1/4 teaspoon nutmeg
zest from 1 orange
3 eggs
2 teaspoons vanilla bean paste
1 hachiya persimmon, puréed
1 stick butter, at room temperature

Orange rum syrup
2 1/2 cups orange juice
1/2 cup water
1/3 scant cup rum
(or more if you like it really strong)
1 scant cup sugar

Instructions

How to make baba dough

Warm the milk to 95 degrees, then mix in the yeast. In a stand mixer or a bowl, add the flour, sugar, salt, nutmeg, and orange zest. Mix well. Make a well in the mixture, and add your eggs, vanilla, persimmon, and milk-yeast mixture. Mix well until the dough forms. (You might need a touch of flour if the dough is extremely wet.)

Cover and allow the dough to rise for about 2 hours. You can deflate or punch down the dough, and using a dough hook on your stand mixer, stir in the softened butter until it has been completely incorporated. Fill buttered baba molds (popover molds will work) to 3/4 of their height. Cover again, and allow to rise another 45 minutes.

Preheat your oven to 400 degrees, then turn the oven down to 350 degrees. Place the babas into the oven. Bake for roughly 20 minutes, or until golden brown. Take them out and allow them to cool.

How to make orange syrup

Place all the ingredients into a pot and bring it to a boil. Turn down the heat and simmer for 7 minutes. Turn the heat off, and allow the syrup to cool. Once it has, place your babas into the syrup. Turn the babas every 10 minutes or so if they aren't submerged in the syrup. Allow them to soak for at least 2 hours. Feel free to add a little more rum here if you like a strong taste.

continued.../

Persimmon and Orange Rum Baba

Sabayon

5 egg yolks
1/2 cup sugar
zest and splash of juice from 1 orange
1/4 cup champagne

Garnish

1 fully ripened fuyu persimmon,
cut into small pieces
2 tablespoons anise hyssop flowers

How to make sabayon

Place the egg yolks, sugar, zest, juice, and champagne into a stainless steel bowl. Put the bowl over a double boiler or a simmering pot of water. Whisk the egg yolk mixture continually until it is thick and airy, but not scrambled. It should take a few minutes for the sabayon to thicken. Take the bowl off the heat. Adjust the seasoning, if need be.

To finish

Make a small cut in the middle of each baba, making sure not to go all the way down to the bottom. Generously spoon the sabayon into the middle of and on top of the baba. Place a little of the syrup onto each plate. Place the baba on top of the glaze. Add the persimmon pieces and anise hyssop.

Chocolate Soufflé with Coffee Liquor

SERVES 8

If you are looking for a light dessert for the chocoholics in your life, this is the one for you. A soufflé is simple to make and dramatic to serve – French desserts 101!

Ingredients

2 teaspoons melted butter
(or as much as needed)

4 tablespoons white sugar
(to coat the ramekins)

2 more tablespoons white sugar
(to mix with the egg whites)

4 ounces 60-percent dark chocolate,
broken into pieces

2 tablespoons butter

2 tablespoons all-purpose flour

9 tablespoons cold milk

1 pinch salt

1 pinch cinnamon

2 large egg yolks

4 large egg whites

1 pinch cream of tartar

1 tablespoon vanilla

3 tablespoons coffee liqueur

vanilla ice cream (optional)

Instructions

Preheat your oven to 375 degrees. Line a rimmed baking sheet with parchment paper. Brush the bottoms and sides of 8 ramekins (5-ounce dishes) lightly with melted butter. Be sure to coat the inside surfaces completely all the way up to the rim. Add 1/2 tablespoon of white sugar to each of the ramekins. Rotate the ramekins until the sugar coats all the interior surfaces. Pour off any extra sugar that doesn't stick to the butter and sides of the ramekins.

Put the chocolate pieces into a metal mixing bowl with the vanilla and coffee liqueur. Place the bowl over a pot with about 3 cups of hot water. The pot should be over low heat. (It can come to a light simmer on low heat, but not a rolling boil.) Melt 2 tablespoons of butter in a skillet over medium heat. Sprinkle in your flour, and then whisk until the flour is incorporated into the butter and the mixture thickens. This should take about 1 minute. Reduce the heat to low, and then whisk in the cold milk until the mixture becomes smooth and thickens. This should take another 2 or 3 minutes. Remove the skillet from the heat. Transfer the mixture to the bowl with the melted chocolate. Add salt and a very small pinch of cinnamon. Mix together thoroughly. Add the egg yolks and mix together.

Put 4 egg whites into another mixing bowl, then add them to the cream of tartar. Whisk until the mixture begins to thicken. (This should take 2 or 3 minutes.) Add 2 tablespoons of sugar in a slow, continuous motion. Continue whisking until the mixture has stiff peaks, which should occur within about 3 minutes.

Fold the egg white mixture into the chocolate mixture in 3 intervals. Mix until the egg whites are thoroughly incorporated into the chocolate base. Divide the combination among your 8 prepared ramekins. Place those ramekins onto the baking sheet. Bake in the preheated oven until the soufflés are puffed and have risen above the tops of the rims. This should take 12 to 15 minutes. Feel free to serve with ice cream or crème anglaise (see page 308).

Sticky Toffee Pudding
with Salted Caramel Ice Cream

SERVES 4

Dates are a real favorite in my house. My sons love picking them out at the farmers market. There are many different varieties, but my favorite is the Medjool. This sticky toffee pudding recipe is basically a date cake with caramel sauce and salted caramel ice cream. The cake is flawless and stays moist for days!

Ingredients

Sticky toffee pudding

3 tablespoons butter, cold, unsalted, cubed (plus more for greasing)

1 teaspoon baking soda

1/4 teaspoon fine sea salt

1/3 cup demerara sugar, plus 1 teaspoon

1/3 cup dark brown sugar, plus 1 teaspoon

2 eggs

3/4 cup flour, plus 2 tablespoons

1 teaspoon vanilla paste

1 cup fresh Medjool dates, pitted

1/2 cup warm water

Patrón caramel sauce

8 ounces brown sugar

4 ounces butter

4 ounces Patrón coffee liqueur

6 ounces cream

Salted caramel ice cream

(see pages 295)

Instructions

How to make sticky toffee pudding

Preheat the oven to 350 degrees, and grease a deep 9-inch by 13-inch baking dish. Add the butter, the baking soda, a pinch of salt, the demerara sugar, the dark brown sugar, the eggs, the flour, and the vanilla paste to a food processor. Pulse until everything is just combined.

Add the dates and the water, and pulse again until the mixture is nearly smooth. Specks of dates should remain visible. Pour the mixture into the baking dish, then bake it for about 30 minutes, or until just firm to the touch. When the pudding has finished baking, remove it from the oven and heat the broiler. Put the rack about 4 inches from the heat source.

How to make Patrón caramel sauce

Put the brown sugar and butter into a small pot. Cook on medium heat until the butter has melted and the sugar has dissolved. Add the Patrón XO Café and flambé it. Let all the alcohol cook off, then add the cream. Whisk the mixture until all is combined. Cook for 1 to 3 minutes, or until you have the desired thickness. Turn off the heat. Set the sauce aside and keep it warm. Pour half the sauce on top of the pudding. Place the cake under the broiler and let it broil until it starts to bubble. Take it out and slice it into individual pieces.

To finish

Place a piece of cake onto each plate. Put a scoop of salted caramel ice cream next to the cake. Spoon some of the extra caramel sauce on top. Serve and enjoy this delicious dessert!

Coffee-and-Donuts
Parsnip Cruller with Coffee Mousse

SERVES 8

What's more American than coffee and donuts? They can be enjoyed any time of the day! People have been using carrots, beets, and zucchini in baked good for years. I put a twist on the classic cruller by adding parsnip because of its natural sweetness. Not feeling adventurous? Omit the parsnip. That omission won't change the delicious outcome.

Ingredients

Parsnips
8 ounces parsnips, sliced
1/3 cup sugar
3 cups water
zest from 1 orange
salt

Pate a choux dough
1 cup milk
1 stick butter
1 tablespoon sugar
1 teaspoon salt
1 cup flour
4 eggs

Coffee-chocolate mousse
1 tablespoon gelatin
2 tablespoons water
1 cup milk
2 tablespoons instant coffee
2 tablespoons vanilla paste
3 egg yolks
3/4 cup sugar (for the egg yolks)
2 tablespoons cornstarch
2 tablespoons cocoa powder
3 egg whites
1/4 cup sugar (for the egg whites)
1 1/2 cups cream
1/3 cup powdered sugar

Instructions

For the parsnip
Place the parsnips, sugar, water, orange, and salt into a small pot. Bring to a simmer and cook for 12 to 15 minutes, or until the parsnips are tender all the way through. (Test with a cake tester.) Strain out the parsnips and reserve them for the pate a choux dough. Reserve the cooking liquid for the finished crullers.

For the pate a choux dough
In a small pot, add your milk, butter, sugar, and salt. Bring to a simmer. As soon as the butter has completely melted, stir in 1 cup of flour with a wooden spoon, and turn the heat down to low. Incorporate all the flour thoroughly and cook for about 1 minute. Transfer the dough to a stand mixer with a paddle attachment. Add the cooked and strained parsnips and run the mixer at medium speed for 1 minute, then turn it down to low speed.

Crack the four eggs into a measuring cup, and add them to the dough one at a time. Make sure each egg is completely incorporated before you add the next egg. Continue until you have added all the eggs.

Place the dough into a pastry bag fitted with a French star piping tip. Cut the parchment paper into 2-inch by 2-inch squares and lay them flat on a sheet pan. Moving the pastry bag in a circular and deliberate manner, pipe a round cruller onto each square. Continue the process until you have no more choux dough. Place the sheet pan with the crullers into the refrigerator for at least 1 hour.

For the coffee-chocolate mousse
In a small ramekin, add the gelatin and water, allowing the mixture to bloom. Meanwhile, place the milk into a pot with the instant coffee and vanilla, and bring the pot to a boil.

Coffee glaze
3/4 cup coffee
1/2 cup sugar

Parsnip glaze
1 1/2 cups powdered sugar
1/2 cup parsnip liquid (reserved when preparing the parsnips)

3 cups vegetable oil for frying

Place the egg yolks and sugar into a stand mixer or mixing bowl. Whisk for 2 minutes, or until the eggs and sugar are light and fluffy. Add the cornstarch and cocoa powder, and mix well. Now add the gelatin to the hot milk blend, stir it in well, then pour it over the egg yolk mixture and mix well.

Clean out the bowl for the stand mixer and use it to whip the egg whites and sugar into stiff peaks. Set aside. Do the same with the cream and powdered sugar to make your whipped cream.

Add the meringue and whipped cream into the coffee-based custard, lightly folding everything together. Once everything is well incorporated, you can either serve the dessert or place the mousse into the refrigerator to chill for at least 2 hours.

For the coffee glaze
Place the coffee and sugar into a pot and bring it to a boil. Turn down the temperature, allowing the pot to simmer for 10 minutes, or until you can glaze a spoon with the mixture. Set the glaze aside to cool completely.

For the parsnip glaze
Mix the powdered sugar with the 1/2 cup of liquid you reserved while preparing the parsnips.

To finish
Add 3 cups of vegetable oil to a pot in preparation for frying the crullers. Set the temperature to 325 degrees. Remove the sheet pan of crullers from the refrigerator. Place 2 to 3 crullers into the fryer pot with the parchment paper still on the crullers. (The number of crullers depends on the size of your pot.) After about 10 to 15 seconds, the parchment paper will release from the donuts, and you can scoop the paper out of the fryer and discard it.

Fry the crullers for 2 to 3 minutes, and flip them over to fry for another 2 minutes. Strain them out and allow them to drain on a sheet pan fitted with a grated rack. Allow them to cool for 2 to 3 minutes, then dip them into the bowl of parsnip sugar glaze. Repeat the process with the remaining donuts. To finish, add a scoop of the coffee mousse to the plate and drizzle some of the coffee glaze on top of the mousse. Add the cruller, serve, and enjoy!

Salted Caramel Ice Cream
with Hazelnut, Chocolate, and Orange

SERVES 8

This recipe was inspired by the infamous Eleven Madison Park restaurant. I've had the pleasure of eating there only once, but the meal definitely left an impression of the level of detail that goes into every aspect of service and preparation for a meal. This dessert is simple in concept, combining caramel, chocolate, hazelnut, and orange. All those flavors go together perfectly! But the result was a plate full of familiar flavors with lots of textures presented in a modern way.

Ingredients

Salted caramel ice cream
1 cup milk

2 cups cream

1/4 cup glucose

3/4 cup sugar, plus another 1/4 cup to mix with the egg yolks

5 egg yolks

salt to taste (up to 1/2 teaspoon)

Aerated chocolate
1/2 cup bittersweet chocolate, plus 2 tablespoons

4 teaspoons grape seed oil

2 iSi cartridges

Honey ganache
1/2 cup heavy cream

1/4 cup honey

7 ounces bittersweet chocolate

2 tablespoons butter

1 cup ground hazelnuts

Meringue
2 egg whites

1/3 cup sugar

1/2 cup hot cocoa mix

Instructions

How to make salted caramel ice cream

Set up an ice bath. Warm your milk, cream, and glucose in a small pan on medium heat. Meanwhile, in another pan on high heat, add 3/4 cup of sugar to make caramel, then add the milk-cream mixture to the caramel carefully. In a bowl, mix the egg yolks and 1/4 cup sugar. Stir on high for 3 minutes, or until the egg yolks are light and fluffy, and temper the yolks with the milk-cream mixture. Put all of it back into a pot. Bring the pot to medium heat, stirring continuously until the temperature reaches 170 degrees. Strain the mixture through a fine mesh strainer into a bowl.

Place the bowl into the ice bath and leave it until the mixture has completely cooled. Refrigerate for at least 2 hours, and then add salt. Place the mixture into an ice cream maker to finish the ice cream. Once you are done, place the ice cream into the freezer until ready to serve.

How to make aerated chocolate

Melt the chocolate and oil together, stirring until the mixture is warm and smooth. Fill the iSi container 3/4 full and charge it with two cartridges. Cool the mixture slightly, then dispense the chocolate foam onto an acetate-lined half baking pan. Freeze the chocolate until you are ready to use it, then break it into pieces.

continued.../

Salted Caramel Ice Cream with Hazelnut, Chocolate, and Orange

Hazelnut sponge cake

1/3 cup sugar

1 cup hazelnuts

3 eggs

3 1/2 ounces milk

1/4 cup flour, plus 1 teaspoon

3 tablespoons butter

1 teaspoon vanilla

1 tablespoon Frangelico

2 iSi cartridges

nonstick oil spray

salt

Orange jam

4 1/2 cups orange juice and segments

2 oranges, zested

2 1/2 cups sugar

1 vanilla bean

1 package liquid pectin

1 orange, cut into supremes
(you should have 8 to 10)

How to make honey ganache

Add the cream and honey to a pot and bring it to a boil. Meanwhile, place the chocolate into a heat-proof bowl. Pour the cream mixture over the chocolate, let it sit for 1 minute, and then whisk until it is completely smooth. Next, add the butter, making the ganache shiny and smooth.

Fill half-moon molds with the ganache and place them into the freezer for at least 2 hours. Afterwards, take the ganache out of the molds, putting each half together with another to make one round truffle. Roll the truffle in hazelnut dust. Keep refrigerated until ready to serve.

How to make meringue

Preheat your oven to 200 degrees. Place the egg whites into a stand mixer with a pinch of sugar. Whisk on high speed. After a minute, gradually add your remaining sugar and the hot cocoa powder. Keep whisking until you have stiff, shiny peaks. This takes about 4 minutes.

Place the mixture into a pastry bag with a plain tip. Line a sheet pan with parchment paper and pipe small rounds onto the paper. (I create both small and tiny rounds.) Place the sheet pan into the oven and bake for 1 hour, remove it, and allow it to dry completely (5 minutes). Place the meringue into an airtight container.

For the hazelnut sponge cake

In a food processor or Vitamix, purée your sugar and hazelnuts until what you have is smooth. Add the rest of the ingredients and purée until smooth. The batter should be smooth and somewhat thick, yet still pourable. Pour it into an iSi siphon half way, then charge the siphon with the first cartridge. Take 1 minute to shake very well, and add the second cartridge. Shake again very well to make sure the air gets all the way through the batter.

Spray small paper cups with nonstick oil. Make three holes with a paring knife around the bottom third of each cup, and one hole in the bottom itself. Shake your siphon well, then fill the paper cup about 3/4 full with the sponge cake batter. Place each cup into the microwave for 30 seconds, and flip it so that it is upside down, which allows the sponge cake to continue cooking. Continue with more cups as you need them. Break the sponge cake into little pieces, then set them aside.

Salted Caramel Ice Cream with Hazelnut, Chocolate, and Orange

How to make orange jam

Place the fruit, zest, sugar, juice, and vanilla bean into a large soup pot. Bring it to a boil, then turn down to a simmer. Stir in the pectin with a hand blender to purée everything, resulting in a smooth consistency. Allow the ingredients to cook for another 3 minutes. Turn off the heat and pour the mixture into a container (or fill your sterilized jars).

Fill your jars and seal them with lids. Place the jars into a water bath, completely covering them with water. Simmer for 5 minutes. Place the jars onto a flat surface, allowing the jam to set. Don't move the jars for 12 hours. You should hear the lids pop, and then you will know you have a proper seal.

To finish

Add a little jam to the bottom of each plate, and add 1 ganache truffle to the plate. Break up some of the hazelnut sponge cake and place it around the jam and truffle. Add a few pieces of the aerated chocolate. Add both sizes of the meringue, along with orange supremes. Finish with the salted caramel ice cream.

Stone Fruit and Almond Tart

SERVES 12

Simply summer! That sums up this recipe in two words. This is my go-to recipe when I want a fast and delicious sweet! Puff pastry, almond paste, and fresh stone fruit – that's really all there is to this dish! Make the almond paste and place it into the center of the pastry. Add the fruit, egg wash, and almonds. Bake, and you're done!

Ingredients

Almond cream

1 1/2 cups almond flour

2/3 cup sugar

6 tablespoons butter
(at room temperature)

1 teaspoon cornstarch

2 teaspoons flour

1 large egg, plus 1 additional egg white

1 teaspoon vanilla extract

2 teaspoons almond extract

Stone fruit

3 nectarines, sliced and pitted

4 plums, sliced and pitted

3 white nectarines, sliced and pitted

3 peaches, sliced and pitted

12 puff pastry squares, really cold

sliced almonds

1 egg (for wash)

Instructions

For the almond cream

Place the almond flour and sugar into a food processor and purée for 30 seconds. Add the butter, cornstarch, and flour to the processor. Purée until the butter, cornstarch, and flour are well incorporated. Next, add the egg and the additional egg white. If there are any clumps, you can stop the machine to scrape the sides, but once you've added the egg and the additional egg white, you should have a really smooth and creamy almond cream. Finish with both the vanilla extract and the almond extract. (I usually double this recipe, which gives me extra almond cream I can use to make something else. With one batch, though, you should have enough to fill the puffs.) Put the almond cream into a plastic piping bag and put it into the refrigerator to firm up a bit, but don't allow it get so cold that you can't pipe it out.

To finish

Line 2 sheet pans with parchment paper. Place 6 puff pastry squares on each pan. Pipe one line of almond cream down the center of each puff pastry. Place sliced fruit on top of the almond cream. Continue the process with all of the puff pastry squares. Brush egg wash around the edges of each pastry. Top with almond slices. Place the pastries into an oven preheated to 425 degrees, and bake for 20 to 25 minutes, or until golden brown. You might want to rotate the 2 sheet pans from the top rack to the bottom rack, and vice versa, so that the pastries cook at the same rate. Once they are golden brown, take them out and allow them to cool completely.

Nectarine Tart with Jam and Sorbet

SERVES 8

Nectarines are chock full of antioxidants (including vitamin C), and they just happen to be my favorite stone fruit. This recipe makes their sweetness shine. The nectarine, whether in its natural state, or in the sorbet or jam, is the essence of this amazing dessert.

Ingredients

Nectarine jam

4 liquid cups of white nectarine slices (approximately 8 small white nectarines)
1/2 cup lemon juice
3/4 cup sugar
1 tablespoon pectin powder
1/2 tablespoon vanilla paste

Nectarine sorbet

3 cups water
2 cups sugar
3 cups white nectarines, skin on, pits removed, and sliced
1 lemon, juiced

Tart crust

(see pages 275–276)

Garnish

2 white nectarines, sliced
2 yellow nectarines, sliced
1/2 cup blueberries
1 tablespoon mint or basil leaves, if desired

Instructions

For the nectarine jam

Place the fruit, lemon juice, sugar, and vanilla into a soup pot. Bring the pot to a boil, then turn the heat down to a simmer and cook for 5 minutes. Stir in the pectin with a hand blender so the mixture is smooth or fairly smooth. Let it cook for another 3 minutes. If you are canning, then turn off the heat and fill your sterilized jars; otherwise, let the jam cool completely, then pour it into a container. Chill it for later use.

For the nectarine sorbet

Place the fruit, sugar, and water into a pot and bring it to a boil. Turn the heat down to a simmer and cook for 5 minutes. Turn off the heat, then place the nectarines into a Vitamix. Purée until smooth, straining if desired. Add the lemon juice, then place the mixture into a bowl and cool it completely (at least 3 hours). Pour it into an ice cream machine, following the directions for that machine. Once the sorbet is done, place it into an airtight container to go into your freezer.

For the tart

Follow the instructions for making a tart dough on pages 275–276. For this recipe, I use a rectangular tart mold. Once you have baked and cooled the crust, completely cover the bottom with nectarine jam about 1/4-inch thick. Next, add white and yellow nectarine slices on top of the tart. Finish with blueberries and mint leaves. Slice the tart and serve with a scoop of nectarine sorbet on each plate.

Fine by Finkbeiner

I had just flown into L.A. from Austin and JP texted that we'd have guests for dinner the next evening. I have had the pleasure of preparing meals for politicians, CEOs, royalty, musicians, and movie stars. And on this occasion, a noted food critic.

Food critic

Peter Finkbeiner traveled all over Europe as a child actor. Later in life he went on to author *IN World Guide*, a travel publication that highlights the best of the best hotels and restaurants around the globe. He has critiqued gourmet dining from Copenhagen to Cape Town. I knew I had to be on my A game that night!

Shopping

I headed for the farmers market in Santa Monica the morning of the dinner and found wonderful mini-rutabagas, truffles, fennel, black trumpet mushrooms, and English peas. I had fresh passion fruit and red and golden beets already in stock. Earlier I made some Wagyu Italian meatball that would be perfect for pasta. I bought some black cod for the fish course, and chose duck for the main course. I was ready to go.

Six-course meal

The dinner began with an easy salad of red and golden beets, and everyone raved over it. Next up was a slow-roasted rutabaga served with a luscious béarnaise sauce. I made the tortellini dough for the pasta course from fennel tops (vibrant green), stuffed with Wagyu, and glazed with truffle sauce. For the fourth course, I seared the black cod hard so it had a nice, crunchy crust on top, and then added a melt-in-your-mouth miso velouté sauce. I prepared a smoked duck breast for the last savory course, finishing it in the pan with a foie gras sauce that was absolutely to die for. The finale was a passion fruit Baked Alaska with coconut, white chocolate, and passion fruit curd. Whew! (See the menu on page 303.)

The critique

Compliments from the guests were music to my ears, but I couldn't help but wonder what Peter thought. I didn't have to wait long for my answer. While I was in the kitchen, busy with cleanup, he popped in to thank me for an outstanding meal. I couldn't stop myself – I had to ask, "How would you rate the meal?" He replied, "I would give you the highest rating. This meal stands up to any of the great restaurants around the world." As a chef, I am always looking for validation of my skill level. Peter confirmed to me that I could cook with the best of them, at least on one night! To this day, his words continue to encourage me.

Dinner Menu

FIRST
roasted beet salad with avocado, manouri cheese, and spicy walnut dressing

SECOND
wood-roasted rutabaga with béarnaise sauce and fried skins

THIRD
fennel tortellini stuffed with Wagyu meatball, fennel purée, and Périgord truffle sauce

FOURTH
crispy black cod with trumpet mushrooms, peas, and miso velouté

FIFTH
smoked duck breast with sorrel, cippolini onions, and foie gras sauce

SIXTH
passion fruit Baked Alaska with coconut and white chocolate

Coconut, Basil, and Macadamia Shortbread

SERVES 10

Here is a dessert with a tropical perspective. The sorbet gets its robust flavor from the fresh, young coconut meat while the buttery shortbread gets a great crunch from the macadamias. The combination works surprisingly well with the addition of basil, and it is absolutely refreshing!

Ingredients

Macadamia shortbread
2 sticks butter
3/4 cup granulated sugar, plus
2 tablespoons (to sprinkle on top)
1 teaspoon salt
1 cup macadamia nuts, ground
2 cups flour

Simple syrup
2 cups water
2 cups sugar

Basil syrup
3/4 cup simple syrup
2 ounces basil leaves

Coconut sorbet
2 1/4 cups simple syrup
1 can coconut milk
meat from 4 young coconuts
1 lemon, juiced
salt

Instructions

How to make macadamia shortbread
Preheat your oven to 350 degrees. Using an electric mixer, beat the butter until it is soft and fluffy. Add 3/4 cup of granulated sugar and 1 teaspoon of salt, and mix well. Add the nuts and flour in 3 stages (until just blended). Place the batter onto a half sheet pan. Using your hands or a piece of parchment paper and a rolling pin, spread the shortbread evenly over the sheet pan. Sprinkle a little sugar on top, then place the sheet pan into the oven. Bake for 20 to 25 minutes, or until golden brown. Remove the shortbread from the oven and allow it to cool completely. After the shortbread has cooled, crush a third of it in a plastic bag. Set that aside until ready to use. Use the rest for treats.

How to make simple syrup
Place the water and sugar into a pot. Bring it to a boil and cook for 5 minutes. Cool completely.

How to make basil syrup
Put the simple syrup and the basil leaves into a Vitamix and purée until smooth. Strain, if desired. Set the syrup aside and keep it cool.

How to make coconut sorbet
Add the simple syrup to a blender with the coconut milk and fresh coconut meat. Purée until smooth, then add the lemon juice and a pinch of salt. Chill until completely cold. Place the mixture into your ice cream maker and follow the instructions for the machine. Once you've made the sorbet, place it into an airtight container and place it into the freezer.

To finish
Place some of the crushed shortbread into the center of each serving bowl. Add a scoop of coconut sorbet on top. Using the back of the scoop, make an indentation in the scoop of sorbet. Spoon some of the basil syrup into the indented sorbet. Finish with a few basil leaves.

Vanilla Pavlova with Cara Cara Orange and Candied Buddha's Hand

SERVES 10–12

Pavlova is a baked meringue with a crisp outer shell and a gooey, soft center. I was introduced to this dessert years ago when I had the pleasure of spending an extended period in Australia. One evening I had a dinner at a friend's house. One of the guests was thrilled to prepare and bring the dessert loaded with kiwi and fresh fruit. This is my version of that experience.

Ingredients

Pavlova
8 egg whites
1 vanilla bean, cut in half and seeds scraped out
2 1/4 cups sugar
1 tablespoon cornstarch, plus 1 additional teaspoon
1/2 lemon, juiced

Candied Buddha's hand
1 Buddha's hand, sliced (1/8-inch thick slices)
1 1/4 cups water
3/4 cup sugar

Instructions

For the pavlova
Preheat your oven to 350 degrees. Add the egg whites and vanilla to a stand mixing bowl. Beat the egg whites until soft peaks start to form, then slowly add the sugar. Continue beating until the meringue is stiff and shiny. This should take 3 to 4 minutes. Next, fold in the cornstarch and lemon juice. Once the ingredients are well incorporated, put the meringue into a pastry bag with a plain tip. Pipe individual meringues onto a sheet pan lined with parchment paper. Place the sheet pan into the oven, and immediately turn the temperature down to 300 degrees. Cook for 1 hour. Turn the oven off. Allow the meringues to cool completely while still in the oven, but with the door open.

For the candied Buddha's hand
Bring a small pot of water to a boil. Place the sliced Buddha's hand into the boiling water. Blanch for 3 seconds, and then strain off the water. Repeat these steps two more times, blanching and straining the Buddha's hand slices. When done, add the water and sugar, and bring to a boil. Put the blanched slices back into the pot. Cook for 5 to 10 minutes. Pour the contents into a preserve jar and seal it properly.

continued.../

Vanilla Pavlova with Cara Cara Orange and Candied Buddha's Hand

Orange sorbet

2 1/2 cups water

2 cups sugar

4 cara cara oranges, peeled and deseeded

zest from 2 cara cara oranges

Crème anglaise

1/2 cup whole milk

1/2 cup whipping cream

1 vanilla bean, cut in half and seeds scraped out

yolks from 3 large eggs

3 tablespoons sugar

1 cup cara cara orange segments

basil leaves

For the orange sorbet

Put the water and sugar into a pot and bring it to a boil. Turn the heat down to a simmer, and then cook for 5 minutes. Turn off the heat and allow the sugar water to cool completely. Once it has cooled, add the oranges and orange zest to the sugar water, then purée it. Strain the mixture, if you desire. Pour the purée into an ice cream maker and follow its instructions. Once the sorbet is done, place it into a container and store it in the freezer.

For the crème anglaise

Combine the milk, heavy cream, vanilla bean, and seeds into a medium saucepan. Bring the mixture to a simmer, then remove it from the heat. Meanwhile, whisk the egg yolks and sugar in a medium bowl until they are blended. Gradually whisk the hot milk-cream mixture into the egg yolks and sugar, forming a custard. Return the custard to the saucepan, stirring it over low heat until it thickens. (Test this by drawing your finger across the back of a spoon. If the custard is thick enough, you should see a clear path where your finger crossed.) This should take about 5 minutes. Do not boil the custard. Strain it into a bowl, and then cover it and chill it. (You can prepare this custard – or crème anglaise -- 1 day in advance.)

To finish

Place a spoonful of crème anglaise onto the bottom of each plate. Add one pavlova, putting it on top of the crème anglaise. Add the orange segments and the candied Buddha's hand around the pavlova. Put the sorbet on top. Finish with basil leaves.

a: who's been into the cake?

b: with my lovely wife and partner in life, Kelly

c: my boys getting feisty while I shop at the market

d: with my brother, Jeff, and Mom and Dad

e: my boys painting the garden red with plum juice

f: kidding around with my brother, Jeff

g: in my younger days

h: climbing to reach the fruit in a mulberry tree

i: cooking at my first catering

BASICS

Basic Egg Pasta

Ingredients

2 3/4 cups flour, plus 1 cup for dusting
3 eggs
3 egg yolks
splash of water
1 teaspoon salt

Instructions

Place the flour into a bowl. Make a well in the center of the flour. Add the eggs, yolks, water, and salt. With a fork, stir the flour mixture until it starts to form a ball of dough, then use your hands to finish forming the dough. Add more flour if the dough is wet. Knead the pasta for 5 to 10 minutes. Cover it and allow it to rest for at least 30 minutes. Use this recipe for different pastas.

Note: Add 1 to 2 tablespoons of different purées to make different colored or flavored pastas.

Semolina Pasta

Ingredients

3 cups semolina
1 1/4 cups warm water
salt (optional)

Instructions

Place the semolina into a bowl and make a hole or well in the center. Add the water and mix with your hands until a dough begins to form. Knead the dough for 10 minutes, or until it is smooth, then wrap it and allow it to rest.

Charred Tomato Butter

Ingredients

6 tomatoes, grilled
1 tablespoon olive oil
1/4 cup cream
1 stick butter
4 fresh basil leaves
salt and pepper

Instructions

Cut the tomatoes in half, drizzle them with olive oil, and season them with salt. Place the tomatoes onto the hot part of the grill and grill them for 3 to 4 minutes, or until charred a bit. Place the grilled tomatoes into a small pot and add cream. Cook for 5 minutes on low heat, then transfer the mixture into a Vitamix with the basil. Purée until the texture is smooth. Slowly add the butter to the blender until all is incorporated. Season with salt and pepper, and keep warm.

Jalapeño Cilantro Pistou

Ingredients

1 bunch cilantro
1 jalapeño pepper
1/4 cup pumpkin seeds, toasted
1 1/4 cups olive oil
1 teaspoon salt

Instructions

Place all the ingredients except for the olive oil into a blender. Purée everything, and then drizzle the oil into the blender in a steady stream until you have a smooth, green sauce. Season with salt and set aside.

Black Garlic Ketchup

Ingredients

4 tablespoons olive oil

1/2 onion, sliced

3 portobello mushrooms

3 1/2 ounces maitake mushrooms

8 ounces balsamic vinegar

8 ounces molasses

6 cups mushroom stock

1/4 cup sugar

5 ounces black garlic

salt

Instructions

In a medium-sized pot, add the oil, onion, mushrooms, and a pinch of salt. Cook for 10 minutes, then add the rest of the ingredients. Bring to a boil, and turn down to a simmer for 30 minutes. Using a hand blender or a Vitamix, purée the sauce until it is silky smooth. Add salt, if desired, set aside, and keep warm.

Basil Pesto Sauce

Ingredients

1 clove of garlic
(feel free to add more if you like garlic)

1/2 ounce Parmesan cheese

1/3 cup roasted pine nuts (I substitute pumpkin seeds for people with nut allergies)

4 ounces fresh, sweet basil

1 1/4 cups extra virgin olive oil

salt

Instructions

Place the garlic, cheese, and nuts (or seeds) into a food processor. Purée for 15 seconds, then add all of the basil leaves. Purée for another 15 seconds. Drizzle in the olive oil while the processor is still running and keep it running until you have a smooth paste. (If you want a thicker pesto, use less oil. If you want runnier sauce, use more oil.) Season with salt and set aside.

Poblano-Nasturtium Sauce

Ingredients

4 poblano peppers
2 cups nasturtium petals
1 1/2 cups Vegenaise
1 1/2 teaspoons salt

Instructions

Char the poblano peppers, either on a gas stove, in a broiler, or on a grill, for 4 to 5 minutes. You want to char the outside of the peppers without making them completely disintegrate.

Once the peppers are charred, allow them to cool. Once they have, peel the charred skin off and remove the seeds. Place the pepper into a Vitamix, along with the nasturtiums and Vegenaise. Purée until smooth, season with salt, and set aside.

Gochujang Aioli

Ingredients

3 tablespoons gochujang paste
1 cup Vegenaise or mayonnaise

Instructions

Place the ingredients into a bowl and mix well. Season with salt, if need be. Set aside until you are ready to use.

Chimichurri

Ingredients

1 1/2 cups fresh Italian parsley leaves
1/2 cup fresh oregano leaves
2 cloves of garlic, minced
1/4 teaspoon red chili flakes
2 tablespoons sherry vinegar
(or red wine)
1 1/2 cups extra virgin olive oil
1 1/2 teaspoons kosher salt

Instructions

Using a chef's knife, chop the parsley and the oregano semi fine, then place them into a bowl. Grate the garlic into the bowl. Add the rest of the ingredients and mix well. Adjust the seasoning, if need be. This chimichurri is great on just about anything.

Green Garlic Oil

Ingredients

3 to 4 stalks green garlic, blanched
1 1/2 cups vegetable oil
salt

Instructions

Chop the green bottoms and tops of the garlic. Put the green garlic into boiling, salted water (1 tablespoon of salt, 4 cups of water) for 45 seconds, then shock the garlic in an ice bath. Squeeze the green garlic dry and place it into a Vitamix with the oil. Purée for 30 seconds to 1 minute, then strain through a chinois. (If you want no sediment in the oil at all, use a cheesecloth as well.) Season with salt, and place the oil into a squeeze bottle.

Salsa

Ingredients

4 large jalapeño peppers or serrano peppers
3 large heirloom tomatoes
1 onion
2 tablespoons olive oil
1 cup water
1/3 cup cilantro
salt

Instructions

Place the jalapeño peppers, tomatoes, and onion into a heat-proof pan. Drizzle with olive oil and season with salt. Place into a broiler preheated to 550 degrees. Broil for 25 to 30 minutes.

Everything on top will look burnt, and that's okay. That gives the sauce a smoky flavor. Remove everything from the broiler and place it into a blender with the water and cilantro. Purée, then season with more salt. Set aside until you are ready to use.

Chive Oil

Ingredients

2 large bunches chives, blanched
1 1/2 cups vegetable oil
salt

Instructions

Follow the directions for the *Green Garlic Oil* on this page, except blanch the chive oil for 15 seconds rather than 45 seconds.

Ramen Broth

Ingredients

3 ounces ginger, sliced
1 whole onion, sliced
1 stalk leek, sliced
2 whole carrots, sliced
2 tablespoons sesame oil
1 whole serrano pepper, sliced
8 cloves of garlic, sliced
1/2 cup soy sauce
1/4 cup mushroom soy sauce
2 tablespoons soybean chili paste
2 tablespoons fermented black bean paste
1 teaspoon sambal
3 pounds chicken bones, roasted
2 pounds beef bones, roasted
10 cups water

Instructions

Put the ginger, onion, leek, and carrots into a pot with the sesame oil and cook for 10 minutes. Next, add the serrano pepper and the garlic. Cook for another 3 minutes, then add the rest of the ingredients and bring the pot to a boil.

Turn down the heat and allow everything to simmer for a few hours. Once you have a deep, rich, flavorful broth, it is ready. If it doesn't taste great, you can reduce it more, or you can adjust the seasoning.

Note: If you want a shorter version, follow the same instructions, but replace the water and the bones with chicken stock. (See *Chicken Stock* on this page.)

Chicken Stock

Ingredients

3 carrots, chopped
1 onion, chopped
1 whole garlic bulb, cut in half
1 bay leaf
4 stalks celery, chopped
2 whole chicken carcasses, raw or roasted
1 gallon water
(or enough to cover everything in the pot)
3 sprigs of fresh thyme
1 tablespoon black peppercorns

Instructions

Place the carrots, onion, garlic bulb, bay leaf, celery, chicken bones, water, peppercorns, and thyme into a large stockpot. Put the pot onto the stove and bring it to a boil. When it boils, lower the heat so you have a slow simmer. Reduce for 3 hours, or until the stock has only half the liquid remaining.

Note: For a dark-colored chicken stock, roast the bones and vegetables. For a light-colored chicken stock, use raw bones and don't roast the vegetables.

For reduced chicken stock, cook the liquid down another 50 percent.

Vegetable Stock

Ingredients

1 onion, charred

2 leeks

3 stalks celery

4 carrots

2 parsnips

1 celeriac

1 cup mushroom stems (if you have them)

5 cloves of garlic

2 bay leaves

1 sprig of thyme

8 cups water

Instructions

Place all the ingredients into a pot and bring it to a boil. Turn the heat down to a simmer, and reduce by half, or until the water tastes flavorful. Strain out the vegetables and discard them. Season the stock with salt.

Whipped Cream

Ingredients

1 cup heavy cream

1/3 cup confectioners' sugar

1 teaspoon vanilla paste

Instructions

Place the cream into a stand mixer and whisk on medium speed for 2 minutes. Add the powdered sugar and vanilla, then whip until the mixture has thickened and has stiff peaks. This should take about 1 additional minute.

Acknowledgements

In no particular order, thanks to all of my past chefs who have shown me ways to prepare food and taught me the habits that make it possible to do my best.

Thanks to Kelly for being the wife of this chef, something that is not easy to do. Even though I no longer work all the crazy hours I worked at restaurants, there are still plenty of long days, travel days, and days she is alone with our boys.

Thanks to my parents, Jim and Judy Servidio, for loving and believing in me, and for teaching me the way to live. (I'm still learning this with my own family.) My parents gave me a foundation based on putting God first.

Thanks to God for calling me into His family, and for giving me this passion and opportunity to do the best I can with it.

Thanks to my brother, Jeff Servidio. I couldn't have done what I've done without him. He has really been there for me, supporting me for a lifetime. I lived with him for about three years when I moved to Austin, and that allowed me to establish myself while living rent-free. So I owe him more thanks than I can ever repay him.

Thanks to my friend (and the best cook I know), Sarah Slaughter. Like my brother, she has been through thick and thin with me, not just during my catering years, but through life in general. I wouldn't be where I am without her help and support. So thank-you!

Thanks to my friend Wayne Solum for all his hard work. His photographs got me started with my website years ago, and a few of his photos appear in this cookbook.

Thanks also to Justin Harvey. The photos of me in the garden are his.

Thanks to Mary Hendren for editing the infant rounds of this book without any direction or help.

A big thank-you to the rest of my family, especially the Bishop sisters with their input and proofing.

Thanks to JP and Eloise for allowing me to grow and for keeping me employed all these years. It is not an easy thing to cook for people on a consistent basis without them getting tired of your cooking, and even tired of having you in their space regularly.

Thanks to Brad Dobson for giving Eloise my name so many years ago. Working for JP and Eloise has been such a huge blessing for me and my family.

A big thank-you to Bill and Rennie Palmer. I absolutely couldn't have done this without them! They have been patient with me throughout my hectic schedule. Bill's editing and Rennie's graphic design have turned my project into something that makes me proud, so a huge thank-you to them.

And thanks to everyone else who has helped me, but who is not mentioned by name.

Index

On the box: 12 DRY PINTS — PRODUCT OF U.S.A. — 2-4 LBS. — **Strawberries** from **CALIFORNIA**